Stormin' Norman

Sermons of the
Reverend Norman E. Stockwell

Volume 3
The Gospel of John

Compilation and Commentary by
Peter Stockwell

Published
by
Westridge art
PO Box 3847
Silverdale, WA 98383

First printing 2020
Copyright by Peter Stockwell
All Rights Reserved

No part of this book may be reproduced, scanned, or distributed in any printed or electronic form without permission.
Do not encourage or participate in any act of piracy or copyright infringement in violtion of the author's rights.
Purchase only authorized editions.

20 10 9 8 7 6 5 4 3 2 1

ISBN: 978-0-9983558-0-1

Printed in the United States of America

Cover and Interior design by
Westridge Art

Ditributed by
Westridge Art
PO Box 3847
Silverdale, WA 98383

Reverend Norman E. Stockwell
March 28, 1916 - July 17, 1986

Norman Stockwell was born in Timmons, Ontario, Canada on March 28, 1916 to Frank and Eva Stockwell who had emigrated from England. After his family moved to the United States, he grew up in North Adams, Massachusetts, He was the middle child of the family. He had an older sister, Dorothy, and brother, Alfred, and two younger sisters, Midge and Mary.

He became an Episcopal priest in 1943 and served in various congregations throughout Idaho and Washington. He married Jane S. Nickolds on February 13, 1943. They departed Massachusetts for Gooding, Idaho. He oversaw four church congregations in Gooding, Jerome, Wendle, and Shoshone, Idaho.

Toward the end of World War II, he worked with the United States Navy in Longbeach, California as a chaplin. He returned to Massachusetts for a short time, but was called to become the rector of St. Marks in Moscow, Idaho where he was also the chaplin for the University of Idaho.

After eight years Norman accepted a position at Church of the Ascension in Twin Falls, Idaho. With an expansion of the facility to provide a larger parish hall and classroom space, the church attendance increased. His ministry continued to grow.

Another eight years precipitated a call to move to Longview, Washington and St. Stephen's Episcopal Church. He remained the rector for another eight years. His final parish was in Bremerton, Washington at St. Paul's Episcopal Church. He retired in 1981 and settled into a comfortable life of travel and supply at various Episcopal churches.

Health issues forced him to a more leisurely life of traveling until a stroke in September of 1985. After ten months of care by his family, he died on July 17, 1986.

He left behind his entire ministry of sermons and papers, some of which are shared in this book of the Gospel of John. Each volume of Stormin' Norman reflects the ministry of a man devoted to improving the lives of other people.

Commentary by Norman's son, Peter Stockwell, will address the current issues and possible relationship to the message of the sermon. Contact him at stockwellpa@wavecable.com

Follow him on Facebook, Instagram, and Twitter.

Believe in the redeeming powers of love as taught by Jesus of Nazareth.

Table of Contents

Wedding at Cana	1
A Drink of Water	5
Signs and Wonders	9
Feeding the 5000	14
The Blind Man	21
The Light of the World	25
Mystery of the Christian Faith	31
Without Me	36
jesus Dispirited	41
Not servants...Friends	45
Death and Resurrection	51
Mary and Martha	55
Who is Jesus Christ?	59
Negativism to Positivism	63
Biography of John	71
About the Author	73
Other Works by Peter Stockwell	75

Editor's note: Parts of Father Stockwell's sermons have some changes to correct minor syntax errors.

Wedding at Cana

On the third day, a wedding took place at Cana in Galilee. Jesus' mother was there, and Jesus and his disciples had also been invited to the wedding. (John 2:1-2)

Commentary

Weddings are a celebration of the hopes and dreams a couple pledges in their lives to each other. They invite friends and family to witness the magnificent event. A reception usually happens after the ceremony, and dinner or hors d'ouvres are served to the guests. One staple of many wedding ceremonies is wine. Although my wedding to my wife Sandy occurred many years ago, I remember the people of St. Paul's Episcopal Church in Bremerton, Washington providing ample bottles of wine for those guests who preferred it. We also had coffee and tea and other drinks for children.

A short time before writing this commentary for my father's sermon, one of my grand-nieces married her long-time beau. Her Uncle Sean, an Episcopal priest in Portland, Oregon, performed the marriage ritual. My nephew wore a stole my father had owned. Friends and family delighted in the union of two young adults, and then the reception and dinner added to the evening's happiness.

The Wine was served and did not seem to run out. Enough spirits were available to sate the palates of a couple of hundred people. At dinner, we had wine. When a bottle on the table ran out, another bottle showed up. No one had to lament running out of wine.

I can imagine the host's embarrassment at the wedding in Cana attending by Jesus and his mother when his supply of wine ran dry. A reputation is an integral part of one's life, and nobody wants it to be negative. The master of the banquet could have ruined any future business by not supplying enough wine.

Jesus caused water to become wine, and the reputation of the master of the banquet survived. My father's sermon is not about the chemistry or physical process of making wine. He centers on the spiritual aspects of the miracle of water into wine without the months of grape growing, harvesting, and production methods to make it.

Sermon

How many of you remember your wedding day? I remember mine 31 years ago. We had the worst blizzard of winter in 1943. But the day was a glorious, happy, beautiful event, even though I was so nervous I hardly knew what I was doing. I am sure of one thing - everyone had a good and joyous time. I'm sure this pleased the Lord and was the reason He was at the wedding in Cana.

In one sense of the word, the episodes of the marriage at Cana is the front piece to the Gospel - summing up pictorially what is to come: how our Lord enters into people's troubles; how he suffices in every difficulty; and above all how he enriches every day for us. What water is to wine, so is any other life compared to the fullness, adventure, and life that Jesus gives us.

There are many wonderful lessons to be learned from this miracle of Cana. Without going into the literal and physical facts, let us look at the spiritual miracle. First is the fact that Jesus was at the wedding. They wanted Him there. They had no fear that He would be out of His element, or fail to fit in, or make others uncomfortable.

Christ does not hold Himself aloof from innocent human happiness - a fact which many of his followers have forgotten with tragic results. People have made Jesus' religion an austere thing, and by their caricatures of him have scared many from Him. It is said that St. Teresa disliked "gloomy People" and prayed to be delivered from "frowning saints." She was right. Our Lord wants us to live life in all its abundance and to be filled with His spirit every moment.

Next is the kindness of the mother of our Lord. No doubt, she noticed the whispering and growing embarrassment of the host. She understood at once that something was wrong, and quite possibly, her son could do something about it.

Perhaps more guests had come to the wedding feast than had been expected. There had been a miscalculation. So Mary whispered encouragement to the servants. "Do whatever He tells you."

This confidence of Mary in her son could only have come out of the long experience of one always unselfish and thoughtful and dependable, always unfailing and generous in helping. Hasn't that been our experience? Having stayed close to our Lord through the years - we know He is always at hand to help.

At the wedding at Cana, Jesus illustrates to us very vividly that one of the prerequisites of true religion is helpfulness - all areas of life: Home, community, work, and recreation, etc.

"Religion that is pure and undefiled before God, the Father, is this: to visit the orphans and widows in their affliction and to keep oneself unstained from the world. (James 1:27)

The next great lesson we learn from the wedding at Cana festivities is:

a) Jesus brought in the servants as His fellow workers.

b) To this very day, Jesus does not keep the healing and helping in His own hands, but offers a share in that to all who will accept it from Him.

c) When we talk about involvement as Christians, this is just what we mean. Helping Christ with His work - not only in the fellowship of the Church - but in the community- in our jobs, our homes, and our recreation.

Indeed, most of us can work for Him in the main by little more than the honesty and thoroughness and cheerfulness with which we carry out our daily tasks - serving man- but only through our Lord Jesus Christ.

The reply that Jesus gives His mother sounds almost like a rebuke - even harsh. What does it mean?

a) We have our Lord's repeated assurances that we possess the fullest right to go to God and tell Him all our problems, troubles, and needs. It really matters to Him what becomes of us and how we fare. Nothing troubles us that is not of interest to Him.

b) Yet in our prayers, we can often be unbelieving. Do we not often speak to God as though He had forgotten, and we have to remind Him what He ought to do? Do we not lose patience with His methods?

c) His mother seemed to slip into this error. Quietness and patience is one of the most difficult of all Christian graces.

The main lesson we learn in this wonderful account of the Wedding at Cana is that Christ brings with Him and offers to anyone who will accept it, a life of abundance, a peace that passes all understanding, a fullness of joy for living, and a supplement of needs which astounds us.

Here is the thing which the whole world has been seeking and it works. With Christ, and in Christ, life grows satisfying and successful and exciting beyond measure.

The only way in which we shall win the world for Christ is by convincing those outside that we have something infinitely valuable that they lack. Then they will come running for a share of it. That we do possess such a thing is the Truth. Sit down with vividness in this telling account of the Wedding at Cana.

Given at St. Paul's Church, Bremerton, WA January 16, 1977

A Drink of Water

When a Samaritan woman came to draw water, Jesus said to her, "Will you give me a drink?" (John 4:7)

Commentary

After working in my yard or repairing parts of my house, I can feel tired and thirsty. Getting a glass water from the tap in the kitchen or a bottle of water from the refrigerator, I can refresh my body and quench my desire. I can imagine Jesus wanting water after a hot, dusty walk from Judea to the well at Sychar.

Discrimination is an ugly and ancient activity of humans around the world. As I write this commentary about the Samaritan woman who met Jesus at the well, many people in the United States are embroiled in demonstrations of marches and confrontations with authorities because of the death of a Minneapolis father of two by police officers. He did not have to become another victim of the brutality of white men against black men.

Jews and Samaritans did not mingle because the Jewish population considered them inferior and unworthy of attention. Discrimination reigned two thousand years ago as much as it does today. We are subject to the learning we attain by our families and friends, and we perpetuate the same biases we foster growing up in the environment in which we live.

Slavery across the world fosters feelings of superiority by the slaveholders and inferiority with the emprisoned populations. Such emotions caused divisions within the political parties and drove our country into a civil war in 1861. Today, people are again agitating for civil war. The civil disobedience and demonstrations call out the need for calm and reform.

Jesus' conversation with the Samaritan woman provides us

an example of what we can be as we mingle with people different from us and yet alike. He proffered an image of truth and honesty the woman accepted and shared with others within Sychar. He treated her to living water that quenched thirst forever. A thirst many of us do not know or have not experienced.

Can we become more like the ideal Jesus represented when he spoke with the Samaritan woman? We are not so different from each other regardless of skin color, race, or socioeconomic status.

Sermon

Having fulfilled your duties to the best of your abilities - have you ever felt weary? Or have you ever felt there were more demands on your life than you felt you could accomplish? You are not alone.

Even our Lord felt this at times. Today's Gospel tells of such a time. Jesus and His disciples had been on the road - teaching, healing, comforting. They came to Sychar at noon, hungry and tired. The disciples went in search of food, and Jesus, weary with all His responsibilities, sat at Jacob's Well.

It seems to me that this is really good news to us. We often think of Jesus as Almighty, the Conquerer, the strong and invincible. But here we learn that, as a man, he too is like us. He got tired. You and I get tired - and see no prospect of anything else. So a tired Christian can understand - might help - as no other person could.

We're so busy sometimes running around in circles we wear ourselves out.

I knew a woman once who had to confront a day of disaster. She faced it valiantly with never a whimper or complaint. She lent all her energy to straightening things out.

A very pious person clad in soft furs and finery dropped in to see her. Her comment was: "Isn't it sweet to know all is in God's plan. The woman knew her life was in God's plan and accepted it as such. But later, she said: "that good pious soul will never know how nearly it was also in God's plan that I should slap her hard." A normal reaction.

Yes, faithful souls who labor and are heavy laden well know that Jesus is carrying far heavier burdens than our own and can show us how to carry ours with courage and quiet heartedness.

So Jesus, tired, sat at Jacob's well resting. A woman came to draw water. Usually, the women of the village came in the cool of the evening. Maybe, because of her unsavory reputation, this woman was unpopular, so came at noon when she would be alone.

Jesus said, "Give me a drink."

Isn't it true what draws most people to Jesus Christ is not so much what he can give us as that which He asks of us?

Christ calls us to serve: to be a brother to the tired, the needy, the lost, the lonely, those in despair. "In so much as you have done it unto to the least of these my brethren ye have done it unto me."

Jesus says, "I accept it from you, gratefully, as a personal kindness to me." So, we too can hold a cup of cool water to Christ's lips, make Him less tired, and be helpful to Him.

You will notice in all the Gospel accounts that Christ never makes use of His own powers to meet His own requirements or those of His friends. The feeding of the 5000 - He depended on those in the crowd. When His disciples were hungry, they had to go and seek food and pay for it as anybody else.

Christ will not do for us what with a little ordinary power and trouble we can do for ourselves. And yet so many expect Christ to miraculously and without effort to solve all problems. The entire road of life has to be traveled foot by foot, one step at a time.

Though the Holy Spirit is the Comforter, the friend in need, He will not spoil or coddle us. And Christ will not use His powers to make good what is lacking to us because of our own crass laziness or unfaithfulness.

The Samaritan woman at the well is taken aback by Jesus' request for a drink. "Jews have no dealings with Samaritans," she said.

To which Jesus replied, "If you only knew."

Oh, what does that mean to us? If we only knew. How foolish our conduct is at times. How false some of our desires are. How Pathetic to reach for the riches of the world. How senseless is our way of life at times. How miserable our rationalizations sound. How foolish our excuses.

Jesus says to us as He said to the Samaritan woman - The

things of this world are transitory, often meaningless - and do not last. I can give you the fulfillment of your soul's desire. You shall never thirst or hunger again, That is a bold claim to make, and yet Christ makes it constantly and with assurances.

And for faithful, dedicated Christian people, Christ arouses in us a longing, a hunger for Him. He is the answer to life and its tired way. There is no growing tired of Christ, no thought of seeking elsewhere for a fuller satisfaction than He gives.

Anyone who lives in Christ and with Christ has in His heart a "spring of water" that is unexhaustible. A peace that passes all understanding, a joy deeper and more real than any other joy, a life more abundant than anyone can know, a power that can meet every call upon life, a perpetual fountain, clear and clean, cooling and refreshing.

"Oh, if you only knew," says Jesus.

Given at St. Paul's Church, Bremerton, WA. February 26, 1978

Signs and Wonders

"Except ye see signs and wonders, you will not believe." (John 4:48)

Commentary

"Except ye see signs and wonders, ye will not believe." Wow. What a statement to make about the faith of people around the globe. Are we such naysayers that the only way we have confidence in what we cannot see is to show us what we are not ready to see?

I studied history in college as part of my degree in education. I came to realize I have seen much that people in history had no idea existed. We fly in heavy aircraft using physics principles of lift and thrust. We travel along roadways at speeds people thought unattainable, and we understand the medical phenomenon of bacteria and viruses, unseen to the naked eye.

People are susceptible to an axiom that if I can't see it, I won't believe it. I understand the skepticism of many who do not have faith in what we, as Christians, believe. Jesus provided many opportunities for advancing the idea which drives people of faith. He did not hammer us over the head with it. He acted.

Today's population reacts to the tensions of watching people mistreated and abused by police, neighbors, fellow workers, and political parties that do not share a common interest in the equal advancement of society. A major illness called COVID 19, a pandemic, swept through the world while I wrote the commentary for this sermon. When a man died in Minneapolis, Minnesota, it sparked massive protests marched across these United States. Threats and counterthreats kindled closed minds to offer civil war as a solution.

Signs and wonders did not bring faith to the forefront of the troubles embroiling citizens within the United States of America. People question God's role in the deaths and attacks, the rioting and looting. People of faith had agendas to match what they wanted to believe. And people of little or no faith relied on their abilities and actions to disrupt or to demonstrate.

I believe my father provides a better understanding of why we should have faith without wanting the outward and visible signs and wonders. It provides a scaffolding to support the faith God gives without relying on signs and wonders. Truly believing in something without signs and wonders is unto itself a wonder and a sign of why faith prevails when we need it.

Sermon

In reading the Bible today, one is, at times, quite amazed and dumbfounded at the many accounts of the miraculous actions that our Lord was able to accomplish during His ministry. We read of His giving sight to the blind, hearing to the deaf, raising the dead, and making the lame walk.

In the Gospel for this Sunday, the 21st Sunday after Trinity, we have an account of our Lord snatching from death, at a distance, the son of a nobleman who had come and asked Jesus to work His cure. Jesus said to him, "Except ye see signs and wonders, ye will not believe." The nobleman was a man of faith who believed in his heart that if Jesus would, He had the power to heal his son even without seeing him.

Jesus said, "Go your way. Your son liveth." And the man believed the words that Jesus had spoken to him and went his way. And it was the same hour that the son was healed.

"Except ye see signs and wonders, ye will not believe." Jesus knew the nature of people, didn't he? What divine insight He had into the human heart. He knew that for the normal run-of-the-mill life, there was the tendency to self-complacency, which is measured by the individual when He says, "My power and the might of my hand hath gotten me this wealth." (Deuteronomy 8:17) It is easy to just ride the crest of the wave of life when things are going smoothly. We are prone to take these things of life for granted. This is the testing ground of faith that in the midst of normality and regularity of the daily affairs of life we maintain with vigor and inner consciousness, the ultimate trust in God, which is the bulwark of life.

People like the spectacular. And it is through the spectacular, all too often, that we create a sensational stir to move our people to an acknowledgment of the inner values of life. It is easy to get a hearing from the mob, simply by being different, parading demonstration, or working the unusual. Aimee Semple McPherson, Billy Sunday, Mary Baker Eddy, attracted huge groups of followers, not by adherence to the traditional approach to God, but by pulling off the unexpected. Men and women flocked to see them, not out of faith, but out of curiosity.

It is the easiest thing in the world to create a following by pulling off the unexpected. If you are going to get talked about, do something extremely unusual.

Jesus could have won the entire population of Judea if He so desired. As a matter of fact, the Devil gave Him the opportunity. All He had to do was to go about healing the sick, mending the cripples, and raising the dead. The Devil tried this approach with Jesus, you remember, with his temptations in the wilderness, but Jesus came not to win the hearts of any artificial sort of way, but to bring them to a relationship with Almighty God, the Father, that through faith and courage, would carry them all along the paths of life. Jesus never worked a miracle as a sign of wonder, but always as a merciful act of God. And of course, the only possible means by which a miracle was possible was through faith and belief in the God's healing power for the person in whom the action was taking place. The nobleman believed that Jesus could heal his son, and went away believing, even though he did not know what happened, he didn't need a sign for his faith.

Life, for the most part, is the day in, day out, routine activities which have to be carried out with regularity if our responsibilities are to be fulfilled. There is little of the sensationalism or spectacular in our lives. It is the daily plodding that makes us what we are. Sometimes it's not easy to keep our faith up to the high level that it should be under the circumstances.

"Faith is the substance of things hoped for, and the evidence of things not seen." Faith is the eternal inner power of a man's heart that keeps him in the traces of the responsibililties and duties of his life so that he is a man rather than a mouse. Real faith is the inner fortitude of a man that carries him to his goal and enables him to do those things he does not want to do and leave undone those things he ought not to do. Faith is the ever-present determination that a man has in his heart to fulfill all the requirements God has laid upon him. Faith is the constant acknowledgment of God and the depending upon Him for all the power of life, which is needed.

Faith, in this sense of the word, is the art of holding on to the real things of life despite of our changing moods in the daily routine. That is why faith is such a necessary virtue. Unless you teach your moods "where to get off," you can never be a sound person, much less a good Christian. You are just a creature, dithering to and fro, with beliefs dependent upon the weather and the state of your indigestion.

That is why daily prayers and religious reading and church-going are necessary products of the Christian life. We have to be continually reminded of what we believe, neither this belief nor any other will automatically remain alive in the mind. It must be fed. As a matter of fact, if you examine a hundred people who had lost their faith, I wonder how many of them would turn out have reasoned out of it by honest argument. Don't most people simply drift away? In our normal, regular day by day life, when we have not sensationalism, we have to train the habit of faith.

And the man who has this faith, real faith, has the power to move mountains. And he has it because he remains constant in his duty toward Almighty God. It is a truism that anything worth having is worth working for. That is why a man of faith would never neglect his duty to worship God every Sunday in His church, even if he wanted to. It might not be convenient, you understand, but if he has work to do, he sacrifices something else out of his life that it may be done. He gives up a party. He gets up a little earlier. He stays home in the afternoon -- anything. But he doesn't miss his first obligation, which is that of worshipping his Creator. Of course, the church could make it easier for the individual by conducting sensational circuses with all the component parts, but signs and wonders will not give the faith that is essential to a man to carry him through all the adversities and trials of his normal life. "Except ye see signs and wonders, ye will not believe." But there have been those down through the ages who did believe, and who have faith simply because God is God, and these self-same people have lighted fires of righteousness and truth so that even in this day when evil is rampant, our lives in society are built and regulated according to the Divine revealed truth of Almighty God.

My friends, have and keep your faith. And if you have the faith of a grain of mustard seed, you would turn the world upside down. But it doesn't come by wishful thinking or hoping it comes by constancy, by plodding, by regularity in our fellowship with Almighty God. Faith is a test, not only in your belief in God, all men have this but in the faithfulness and regularity of your communion and relationship with God. Not only in times of storm and stress but in the humdrum existence of normal, day by day living. Faith is not only your belief in God but your being with God in your thoughts and your words and your deeds so that all the actions of your life are regulated by the divine power that lies deep within your heart. For this strength you need, neither signs nor wonders. Out of your faithfulness, when the journey's end has come, you will be able to say with St. Paul, "I have fought a good fight. I have finished my course. I have kept the faith."

Given at St. Stephen's Church, Longview, WA, October 30, 1966
and St. Paul's Church, Bremerton, WA, September 8, 1974

Feeding the 5000

When Jesus looked up and saw a great crowd coming toward him, he said to Philip, "Where shall we buy bread for these people to eat?"
(John 6:5)

Commentary

I'm a believer in the philosophy of knowledge being the best asset we can have in our lives. We learn from the people who have come before us, and we add to the learning as we study and modify what we have already learned. Some concepts are rock solid and need no changes. Some knowledge is in its infancy, and as we mature the learning curve, we discover improvements that make the education better and more rock-solid. Occasionally, we uncover something phenomenal which eluded us. We build on the foundation created by the construction of ideas from the phenomenon.

Sometimes, we are baffled by circumstances that we have observed for centuries and millennia. The event happened, and the report of the occurrence told or written by people has no knowledge base that creates an understanding of what happened. Feeding five thousand people with two small fish and five loaves of bread is such a report.

Being a writer, I can imagine the Gospel writers may have exaggerrated the situation to emphasize the power Jesus had. They may have left out the fact that people carried food with them and shared what they had. Still, most people don't bring food with them when they are rushing around a lake to hear the man who inspired such a trek from their previous encounter with Him. Grocery stores were not an abundant part of the environment.

Why did the story become one of Jesus creating a miracle of stemming the appetites of so many people? While I write this commentary, our country is in the a pandemic brought on by COVID-19, a virus with deadly results and maiming potential. As we have sheltered at home away from other family members and friends, as we have covered our faces when we need to be in public areas, as we avoid other people by maintaining a six-foot space, a miracle of sorts has occurred. We are doing what we can to feed the need for healthy living. The population accepted the idea that the virus could not spread around to us if we agreed with the information we received.

Another mournful event brought about a phenomenon when a man died due to police actions that strangled him on a street in Minneapolis, Minnesota. People wanted to do something about the systemic racial divide cursing our country for 400 years. Thousands marched around the "lake" to hear people express their outrage and anger at the lack of God's love in our lives.

Jesus taught on that desolate grassy hillside after people amassed to hear him speak. He taught them, much as we have been taught these last months and weeks about our fight against two viruses plaguing our country and the world. One virus is a virulent strain of a coronavirus, the other a virulent strain of hypocrisy about our racial differences. Although millions worldwide contracted the COVID-19 virus and thousands died, we worked together for the discovery of new knowledge to stem the tide of the illness.

The other situation is not new to humanity. Racial separation, slavery, and bigotry are as old as human history. We continue to study and modify what we already know to find a cure for our inability to accept we are all God's children.

My father's sermon addresses what happened on that hillside two-thousand years ago. It was a miracle then. It is a miracle today. What we experience with illness and bigotry today can receive the same type of miracle if we are willing to accept new knowledge and understanding that we have an advocate in Jesus Christ. Religious differences are not the problem. We are. Within each of the world's great religions lie the miracles for us to learn and live each day.

Sermon

Back from their tour of the towns of Galilee, into which Jesus had sent them to preach and to heal, came the disciples, telling him all that they had done. Jesus said, "Come, let us go apart into a desert place, and rest awhile." So they launched out in a ship privately to go to the lonely country on the other side of the lake. But the people of the countryside, recognizing Jesus and His men, ran around the shore of the lake and were on the other side when Jesus and His disciples landed. The disciples were doubtlessly annoyed because they had come for a rest, but Jesus looked on these eager people with compassion. They seemed like sheep having no shepherds, and he began to teach them many things.

But as the day fell into evening, the Disciples came to the Master and urged Him to send the people home to buy bread so that they might eat. Jesus said unto them, "Go, give them something eat."

They replied to Him, "Lord, we have only five loaves and two fishes.

The account that follows is written in all four of the Gospels, but it is true nevertheless that we cannot clearly understand it. Here were 5000 people in the wilderness whose hunger Jesus was moved to satisfy. And He fed them the small substance of five loaves of bread and two small fishes. How was it done? We cannot tell. In any case, the significance of whatever it was that happened there in the wilderness is enough to point us the way to the fulfillment of a complete life with God.

Look at the sequence of the parable. First, "They came." The great thing in our spiritual life, and then basically in our physical life, is found in just coming. That great mass of 5000 people had seen their Lord, and although they knew not where He was going, they set out to follow Him. They ran all around the shores of the lake that they might be on the other side when He arrived. They truly came. Consecrated Christians have won the first lap of the race for spiritual life because they have come. We are beginning to see the possibility of a new dawn of peace and calm in the world again because our young men and women were willing and eager to come when the need was great. They knew the cost and sacrifice that would be expected of them. The knew not, however, where the roads of their lives would lead them -- to pain and suffering, agonizing death, broken bodies, or a safe return. But even so, when the call was issued, they came.

The great thing is that we just come. We present ourselves, our souls and bodies, to be a reasonable, holy, and living sacrifice. We cannot predict the future, we cannot see where our lives will lead, but we come, in faith, remembering our Lord's words., "Come unto me all ye that travail and are heavy laden, and I will refresh you." Our life might not be easy, but at least we shall have the strength to meet it honestly and courageously if we come.

When asked by Jesus what was at hand to feed the 5000 people that disciples answered, "Lord, we have only..." Yes, surely, it wasn't much. Five loaves and two small fishes to feed that great mass of people. And yet the disciples in absolute confidence and faith brought those meager offerings to their Lord saying, "Lord, we only have these. But take them and do with them what thou wilt."

Sometimes as we review our circumstances and take inventory of our stock, we find that our resources are low indeed. At least we think so. But the truth is that we all have something to offer. In our eyes, it might seem a paltry contribution to make to God's service. But whatever it is, give it with faith. "Lord, we have only..." Remember that human resources, as meager as they might be, will be plenty with the divine power of God. God can work miracles with the least that we can give Him, but the truth is that unless we do contribute something, no action will be forthcoming. We have to give, and in giving, we get.

When thinking about the Church particularly, we think that the things that we have are especially few. I wonder. Just think of the resources of the Church. "Lord, we have only..." But it is tremendous. We are blessed with the Bible, the most beautiful combination of services the world knows, sacraments -- particularly those of Baptism and Holy Communion, prayer-life, and common fellowship. Could we dare ask for more? The reason we feel fretful and uneasy at times, I am sure, is because we do not use the resources at hand. We say, "Lord, we have only" without thinking actually of all that we do have.

Regardless of what you have and I have, bring them to God. Truly we might only ... but with God's ever-ready help, they will be enough, rest assured of that.

This isn't the end of the story of our Lord feeding 5000 people with five loaves of bread and two small fishes. Yes, the Disciples had only ... but our Lord said, "Bring them to me."

Whatever they are, two small fishes and some bread, our sorrow and agony, our joy, our very life, whatever it is, "Bring them to me."

The disciples did not know Jesus very well; they had not seen Him until He first appeared at Capernaum and began to preach. It was there that he called the first of the Apostles -- Peter, James, and John. But those Apostles knew., at first sight of their Lord, that they had no choice but to follow Him. He, surely, was the "way, the truth, and the life." There was a compelling forcefulness about the glow of His face, a beckoning in His humble body, the power of God in His every word that drew the Apostles to Him like a magnet draws steel filings. They saw the Lord, and in faith they came to Him and gave Him their very all. Does it sound queer to hear that He was able to draw men to Him in such a fashion? Those of you who have come to Jesus Christ, with just little that you have, and have given those small gifts to God, know the answer to the mystery. Jesus Christ is life. He is the way that leads to eternal salvation. But the pre-requisite for receiving the grace of the Divine is responding to the call of the Lord to "Bring them to me." Whatever you might have to offer, whatever might be your contribution, bring it to God, even if it might be only (whatever it is.)

A young, very nervous, and newly ordained minister preached his first sermon to his new congregation. His topic was the parable of the feeding of the 5000. He preached along for a few minutes and then said, "and so our Lord fed a man with 5000 fishes and 2000 loaves of bread. A little boy, sitting in the front pew, retorted, "Hm, that's nothing."

The poor minister was very flustered and could not go on. He vowed that he would preach on the same text the next week, which he did. He got along quite well, and when he finished, he could not resist the temptation to ask the fresh young lad, "could you do that?"

"Sure," said the youngster.

"How?" the minister wanted to know.

"I'd use what was left from last week, "beamed the boy. Even after we have given to the Lord, there is still much left to be given Him.

Jesus saith, "Bring them to me." The truth is that even though we may have only ... it will be sufficient. Our Lord will need nothing that has been left over but will take what you offer in good faith and use it for the service of the Kingdom.

So often, the Church suffers because people are not willing to give. I don't mean financially necessarily, although that is extremely important. No one knows better than a priest how hard it is to get helpers to work in the Sunday School, or do the Altar work, or help keep God's house in order, or sing in the choir or serve on the vestry or Bishop's Committee or do the dozen or so other things that make for a better and more complete fellowship of our Lord's community, the Church. The answer is always the same. "Oh, I don't know anything about that." Or "I have only ..." such little time, meager talents, no abilities, it's not convenient, And so on.

Whatever it be, "Bring it to me." Saith the Lord.

"If God can make -- of an ugly seed,
   with a bit of earth and air,
And dew and rain, sunshine and shade --
   A flower so wondrous fair;
What can He make -- of a soul like you,
   with the Bible and faith and prayer,
And the Holy Spirit -- if you do His will,
   And trust his love and care.
            A.D. Burkett

Five Thousand people sitting on the grass, listening to the words of Jesus. And when the evening was come, rather than send them away hungry that they might faint by the wayside, Jesus told His disciples to feed them. It was done -- with five loaves of bread and two small fishes.

How? Simply because the Apostles had the faith that can

move mountains. They had only..., but what they had they brought to the Master knowing full well that their resources and Divine will, combined, would prove sufficient.

"To whom little is given, from Him, much shall be expected."

Given at Gooding, Shoshone, and Jerome, Idaho, March 18, 1945
At Navy Chapel on June 1, 1945
At St. Thomas on August 11, 1946
At St. Mark's september 8, 1946
At K.R.P.L. February 23, 1948
At Cathlamet, Washington on July 28, 1963
At St. Pauls' Church in Bremerton, Washington on August 15, 1976

The Blind Man

Whether he be a sinner or no, I know not; one thing I know, whereas I was blind, now do I see. (John 9:25)

Commentary

Blindness is not something anyone wants, and yet illness, injury, congenital birth defects contribute to the number of people who are physically blind. I partially share this situation in that I was injured by a large firecracker explosion when I was seventeen. I lost the sight in my left eye. During my stay in the hospital, both eyes were bandaged for a couple of days while the medical staff worked to restore my sight. After two surgeries, one to relieve the unbearable increase of pressure in the injured globe because of the blood flow into the corneal portion of the eye and another to drain more blood from behind the lens, The doctors did not correct the damage done.

I have adjusted to the use of one eye and successfully finished an education at my high school in Minnesota. I received a degree in education and taught for over thirty years in Kitsap County in Washington State. I had begun playing soccer while a high school student and after a year away from the sport to allow healing of the eye, I continued as a college student and an adult to coach, referee, and play.

When I read this sermon and thought about the man born without sight, and the parents who raised him, I could empathize. My mother said I did not have to return to the Episcopal private, residential school I had attended for two years. I responded with an emphatic, "I am returning to school." They agreed to let me

I did not have to become a beggar as the man in this story. My options were not limited because of the loss of sight in one eye. I carried on as if I was physically whole. I did not need a man to make mud and cover my eyes and tell me to wash so I could see. I guess that brings me to what I think of as the other meaning of this story.

Jesus performed this miracle of restoring sight on the Sabbath. Jewish law forbade any work on the day of rest. When the man was brought to the Pharises for questioning about his gaining sight, the confusion and disbelief was great. The argument raged that Jesus must be a sinner, but only a man of God could restore the sight of man born blind.

How many of us are blind, not physically, but in what we observe in this world. Do we see the truth of events dealing with the death of a man at the hands of police? Or the shooting of an innocent woman when her house was barraged by police? Are we blind to the actions of protestors who burn, destroy and loot while others remain peaceful and controlled? Do we lose sight of what we are to become when events run counter to our beliefs? Are we blind to what God has for us as followers of Jesus Christ? Are we like the Pharises and adhere to structures that need rebuilding or simply to be razed?

My Father referenced my niece, who as a child had a hearing problem which disappeared for no apparent reason other than much prayer and what may be intervention by unknown and unseen forces working around us and in us and with us. As the blind man said to the Pharises, "I do not who he is. I can't answer your questions. I know nothing of Sabbath laws. I do not know about sinners. But whereas I was blind, now I see." Have faith, people.

Sermon

Very often surprising things happen to us for which we do not have a logical explanation. They defy our rational minds, or run contrary to our understanding of the universe. My granddaughter's hearing is a good example. This morning's text is another.

I want to think with you, not so much about the miracle, as the facts that lie behind the event. Jewish law said -- No work on the Sabbath. That included healing. Jesus cured the blind man on the Sabbath and was condemned as a sinner. That was confusing. He was a sinner and yet had the power to heal.

Neightbors asked the blind man how he recovered his sight.

He told them of the man named Jesus. They asked, "Who is He? Where is he?" The blind man did not know, but he could see.

He was brought before the Pharises who asked the same questions. The blind man gave the same answers. Finally, there was the skepticism which questions the fact that he was congenitally blind from birth. His parents are brought in and asked about his blindness. If so, then how come he sees now? They said he is of age, ask him yourself.

The Pharises asked the blind man again about Jesus. He responded, "I do not who Jesus is. I can't answer your questions. I know nothing of Sabbath laws. I do not know about sinners. But whereas I was blind, now I see."

This matter hits close to the heart of where each of us lives. How many of us can give a reason for the faith that is in us? I believe but don't know why. Others state they cannot believe anything which cannot be explained in a rational manner. Many aspects of our faith defy logical explanations. The essence of faith is in seeing and believing. I cannot explain how Christ came into my life. Whereas I was blind, now I see.

What things do I see? What things am I sure of? There are a great many, but let us think of just three or four. In the first place, we love. I have asked a great many people for a clear-cut definition of love and have yet to receive one. However, love is one of the most real things in the world. But what is it? It defies definition. Yet it is real and powerful and of eternal certainty. Out of love comes all the good, the true, and the beautiful. And just as we believe in love and cannot really explain it, there are certain aspects of the nature of our faith, which we believe and yet cannot explain why.

If you love, you have discovered the greatest religious truth of all. You know that whereas before you loved, you were blind. Since you have loved, you see.

Another certainty of life that brings us close to God and establishes our faith is "The Sense of Wonder." All of us experience this sense of wonder- - the mountains, a sunset (green flash in Hawaii), the ebb and flow of tides, even the simple things of life.

These things make us wonder. They are real. We know we experience them. We know something happens to that which we call our souls, and we know we are experiencing something divine - something we call beauty.

So after we are in awe and wonder of many things in this world, that very sense of wonder is one of the surest and most certain things we know. It leads us very close to God, and yet we can't explain it any more than we can explain some of the dogma of our faith.

Another certainty that leads us very close to God and yet is so difficult to understand is Prayer. How can any of us say with certainty and meaning "Our Father, who art in Heaven" and not feel that you know the Father and have found the answer to your life?

Anyone who has had any genuine experience with Prayer knows it is real - just as real as love, wonder, and awe. And like wonder and love, Prayer escapes definition.

Why Prayer helps us to see when we are blind, we cannot say - but we do know that it helps us to see and gives answers. You and I know that through prayer, we find God - real, alive, and ever-present. How and why, we cannot say and yet we are so certain of it, that it is a very real part of our lives.

With these three certainties, you need never doubt your faith. Every day of your life, you love a little. Not a day goes by that you are not wondering at things too great for you. And at some time every day, you are consciously or unconsciously praying to your God.

Never mind the Pharisees, the doubters, your neighbors who ask you how these things can be. Remember, once you were blind, and now you see. You now live in the promised hope that you will see all things clearly, much more clearly than ever before.

Thank God for the miracle of sight- both physically and spiritually.

> Given at St. Paul's Church, Bremerton, Washington,
> March 5, 1972 and February 5, 1978

The Light of the World

I am the light of the world. Whoever follows me will never walk in darkness but will have the light of life. (John 8:12)

Commentary

Light is a phenomenon with the properties to brighten our days, illuminate our nights, and provide for the growth of plants. Light produces heat, which warms our bodies and keeps temperatures on this planet at reasonable levels in various parts of the globe. We measure time by following the orbiting purveyor of most of our light, the Sun.

I enjoy bright, sunny days of summer with warms air and long hours. I can accept the shorter days of light in winter because the revolution of Earth around the Sun means a return to the longer daylight hours. All of these things are the physical light elements that spark our ability to exist as living beings on Earth.

The metaphorical light is another matter, and by matter, I do not mean the physical. The word light is used in the English language to signify knowledge, awareness, acceptance, and other things. Jesus is the light of the world. So does that mean anything to us today? I believe that we should be enlightened as to do the teachings of Jesus Christ. Therefore my father preached about the quality of the light.

In this year of 2020, humans are fighting a virus determined to sicken us and alter our physical wellness. We are also fighting an equality battle lingering in the minds and hearts of the population from a 400-year history of enslaving a group of people and after "freeing" them, attempting to keep them in immoral slavery based on attitude.

God's light shines brightly on those interested in "curing" both the COVID-19 virus and the superiority virus running through a segment of society. Jesus Christ is not a forgotten entity of history, nor will He be lost in the hearts of those who decide life in the light is better than the darkness of ignorance and emotional depravity. This year of 2020 has challenged us and offered an opportunity for growth and freedom from oblivion.

I am a cradle Episcopalian, meaning I have been a Christian for my entire life. I have lived in the light for most of it, and I can attest to the idea of a Christ who shares God's love for us. I have lived in darkness, away from the power of a Risen Lord, and I did not do well. I prefer enlightenment over human frailty in the darkness. We should strive for the best in ourselves as we encourage the best in family and friends, in neighbors and strangers.

I keep what my father wrote and delivered as a message worth reading, a message worth hearing, and a message worth living.

Sermon

There are many ways of describing what theologians call "the work of Christ," many ways of expressing how He accomplished the Salvation of men. Some of these explanations are hard to understand and perhaps even harder to accept. None of them has the profound simplicity of the words recorded in St. John -- "I am the light of the world: he that followeth me shall not walk in darkness, but shall have the light of life.

The people in darkness are those of old and those today who know not Christ. For despite all that modern learning and modern sentiment have done to set before us in sympathetic colors the religion of the Gentiles, in times past and in our own, "darkness" remains a true word by which to describe what religion means to the great masses of the world whom the Gospel has never reached. And in darkness, there always reigns confusion and fear. Confusion arises from the mere number of gods and spirits which people the unseen world -- gods of every sort, good and bad. Darker still is the confusion of ignorance, the magic, and superstition that thrive in mental darkness. Worse yet again is the moral confusion that spreads and thickens where there is no clear word from the unseen to light the moral life -- only gods immoral, gods, non-moral, and gods imperfectly moral.

And to confusion in the darkness, there is added fear -- the haunting fear of daily existence. Even more oppressive is a fear of the future, the fear of cold darkness beyond this life.

But paganism is not to be found only in the past nor in heathenism in far-off countries. Our citizens here at home may be enjoying the benefit of a partly Christian society; but, in the full sense, half of them are pagans because they live lives in ignorance of the power of Christ and in complete blindness to His claims upon them. Though these contemporary pagans may think of themselves as enlightened, they, too, are in darkness, and for them, darkness brings confusion and fear.

Far too generally, we take the light of Christ for granted. Not remembering the darkness that reigns in His absence, we do not value its priceless worth, the light which shines with His Advent. It is for the same reason that health seems dearer when we have known long sickness and the homeland more precious when we have borne the pain of exile.

It takes the vast physical universe to impress us with the range and might of God's sheer power, but the fullness of His glory is not visible in the mere display of hugeness nor even in order or beauty. His ultimate and central glory is a moral glory, and His reign a moral reign. In Christ, through whom He gives us light, God shows us Himself openly and willingly and declares in one life all that man can know of Him and at the same time all that He can see in us and that He asks of us. This light not only reveals, but it also cheers and heals. The presence of Him who is light is cheering like the dawn to one who has watched all night. It brightens and invigorates. And like the sun, it cleanses and heals. When the Sun of Righteousness arises, there is healing in His wings.

In the Gospel of St. John, this light that Christ brings is always associated with Life. "The life was the light of men." and "he that followeth me shall have the light of life."

What is meant by life in St. John's Gospel is, of course, not mere human existence. It does not even imply abundant vitality. Nor does eternal life refer to the duration of life: it is a quality of life. It is a divine quality in life and not the indefinite prolongation of life. It is not a certain amount of life, but a certain kind of life.

It is that kind or quality of life which a man possesses who is living in Christ and in whom Christ lives. It is living in Christ that constitutes eternal life. The word "believe" is used in its richest sense when our Lord says, "He that believeth in the Son hath eternal life." In other words, our possession of eternal life depends on our relationship to Christ. If we have accepted Him and given our lives with Him, and He lives in us and we in Him, our mere existence is transfigured so that it becomes eternal life. Its quality has been transmuted and exalted.

Another way of describing eternal life, which we find in the fourth gospel, is to define it as "knowing God." But knowing in this Gospel is always given a rich and mystical sense. To know God is not simply to be aware of His existence: it is not even to know truths about Him. It is to know Him by deep and direct personal acquaintance. Such knowledge goes so far beyond anything merely intellectual; its content is mainly moral and religious. In its fullest form, it is the union of the believer with God through Christ. Such is the meaning of knowledge in the saying: "I am the good shepherd: I know mine own, and my own know me, even as the Father knoweth me, and I know the Father." The true believers, that is, know Christ in something like the deep and intimate sense in which Christ knows God the Father.

In the Gospel according to St. John, Jesus speaks almost exclusively in religious terms, so that in this Gospel, there is taught very little concrete and specific morality. Hence it is easier to give abstract definitions of eternal life in religious terms than to give it free and varied moral content. That content is more easily filled in if we remember that eternal life is St. John's equivalent for the "kingdom of God" in the other three Gospels. The meaning of each is "the kind of life characteristic of men when God rules in their lives." Knowing God, believing in Christ, living with Christ, living under the reign of God, entering the Kingdom of God -- all these are thus different versions or aspects of the same central reality. To conceive Christ as the life-giver and as the Founder of the Kingdom of God is not to assign Him two different roles. It is the same Christ as experienced and interpreted by two different types of religious genius -- the mystical and the prophetic.

It is clear then that eternal life is a present possession. It is not something merely to hope for: it is something to win here and now. We can live in Christ, believe in Christ, and know God at this very moment. Its relationship to life after death is, therefore, one of continuity. Death can only enrich it. Begun here and now, this divine quality of life, once secured, continues forever, never subject to decay or extinction, for it is a treasure beyond the reach of moth and rust.

"If any man be in Christ, he is a new creature: old things are passed away: behold, all things are become new. That is St. Paul's perfect description of the experience of rebirth, of what it feels like when you have completely surrendered to Christ and have been possessed by Him. Whether that conversion was slow in coming or sudden, the result is the same. You feel yourself a new creature. Old things have passed away. What is it that makes the whole world around you shine with an unwonted freshness of color? What is it that creates this glow as of dawn, endowing the commonest objects with a new radiance? First, and foremost, it is because you have met a new friend and have been mastered by Him. The sense of His power and His presence burns within you and fills all your thoughts. It is the joy of this hitherto unknown fellowship, that makes the world a different place in which to live. Your discipleship is so loyally complete, and Christ's point of view is now so wholly yours that the old standards and motives and purposes seem suddenly dull and dead. They have grown colorless and stale. But in their place comes crowding into the center of your life new standards -- His way of judging: new motives -- the longing to serve Him: a new goal of ambition -- the unswerving devotion to His kingdom who said, "Behold, I make all things new."

For the reward of such a new life, the price to be paid is high. The delusion that it is possible to serve Christ without really following Him may be comforting, but it is an error which he never encouraged. He said, "If any man serves me, let him follow me." Yet the error is particularly familiar among those who are intensely devoted to forms and ceremonies and so ecclesiastical minded that pious observances fill the whole of their religious life. It is easy in that case to believe that if Christ is the head of the Church and responsible for many of its ordinances, we are undoubtedly serving Him when we perform its ceremonies and observe its law. But in keeping the rules of the Church can be interpreted as serving Christ, it is certainly not the same thing as following Him, for it is perfectly possible to be piously correct and orthodox and "a good churchman" and still be a stranger to the Spirit of Christ. Serving Christ may come to mean not more than a legalistic adherence to rules and traditions, a Christian form of Phariseeism. But following Christ can only mean acting like Christ -- taking the risks that He took, showing forth the Spirit that He manifested, making the kind of enemies He made, treating people as He treated them, adopting His amazingly unconventional scale of values, and being ready as He was to pay the price of uttermost loyalty. That is the only kind of service that can satisfy Him. He who is the light of the world, the light, without which there can be only darkness, the light which is very life itself.

Given at St. Mark's Church, Moscow, Idaho and Palouse, Idaho,
May 1, 1949
and Church of the Ascenion, Twin Falls, Idaho, September 28, 1958

Mystery of the Christian Faith

Jesus said, "For this I was born, for this I came unto the world, and all who are not deaf to Truth listen to my voice." (John 18:37)

Commentary

I write mysteries about crime and misdeeds by people in my fictional world. I use the area in which I live as a backdrop. I can relate my characters to the places and buildings with which I am familiar. People who live in the same area enjoy seeing references to everday stuff.

My father's sermon mystery is familiar to us, like the streets, buildings, and waterways in my stories. The magic of Christian Faith also has a lot of explaining to do. A person can accept an idea, a notion about the concept that this life is not all there is. Humanity's attempt to explain the world around them started with folklore and the beginning of recorded history.

Why do Christians hold to a belief with no shred of physical evidence other than the writings of a bunch of men two thousand years ago? We accept as fact, these letters and Gospels tell us about a man who lived and taught and preached and promised. The one hard concept for many humans to believe is that He claimed to be the son of God, a God many people will not or cannot fathom without any reliable evidentiary documentation.

That brings me to exploration of my life and how such an influential presence directs what is best for me. As I have written, I am a cradle Episcopalian, born in the church, baptized, confirmed, and raised by staunch Christian parents. I was taught the only way

I know to this day how to live. My Father preached that we learn from those who had a pressure of God in their lives, and we then understand the influence of God in our lives. I celebrate twenty-nine years of marriage to my adorable wife, Sandy, this year of 2020. As it is a second marriage, I felt the pressure of God when I asked for assistance to find someone to marry. I had been single for nearly ten years and was unsuccessful in my pursuit of female companionship, not that I was alone for all those years. I just could not agree on a person to be with me for the long haul.

One day, as I returned from visiting a friend in Olympia, Washington, and deciding our relationship was not viable, I said to God, "I give up trying to find someone. I leave it up to you." That was it. A plea for help with little expectation for an answer. After all, I was on my own, feeling little or no pressure from God.

I attended St. Paul's Church in Bremerton, Washington, where my Father presented this sermon before he retired. My father died in 1986, and this was the same year as my plea to God. My mother allowed me and my son to live in the basement apartment of her house for a nominal rent. I helped her transition through the loss of her husband, my father.

The pressure of God flashed into my life on January 1, 1989, when a woman attended St. Paul's for the first time with two friends. She was newly separated from her husband of 20 years, a Naval flight officer recently stationed at Bangor Submarine Base in Kitsap County. Her male friend was a Naval doctor, and his wife was a librarian. They had met on Guam.

The pressure of God came when a voice sounded in my head with the words, "There she is." The mystery of Christian Faith focused on those three words that had meaning for me. I was the one for her? No expectation existed. We began dating and after her divorce was final, we married in that same church where we met. The pressure of God has been present in my life even when I was not aware of it. The mystery of the Christian Faith had a foundation of acceptance. I believe my conversations with Jesus and with God through the Holy Spirit have pushed me to be a better human and a Disciple of Jesus Christ. I pray you can find solace in my Father's sermon.

Sermon

The mystery of the Christian Faith is Christ in you -- the hope of Glory.

How do you identify the spiritually mature person? Do you consider yourself spiritually mature? Are you an adult in the life of Spirit? Are you standing still, or are you growing? How do you evaluate yourself?

I am not referring to religious knowledge but a religious experience. Do you have a first-hand experience of God? Do you have Christ's truth in you and listen to His voice? These are serious questions for each of us.

Most people who have any sense of the pressure of God in their lives have come to that relationship because of contact with people who themselves have had a deep sense of the pressure of God in their lives. Maybe a parent, a grandparent, a priest, or Godparents.

Or

What experiences have you had in which you have become aware of God? Was it where you came to the end of your rope and knew that there was no power in yourself to help yourself, so you had to turn to some outside Power to get the help you needed?

Or

Perhaps you came to the hospital bedside of a person you loved and knew there was nothing further that could be done -- no operation, no medicine, no doctor. All had been done that could be done. So you put that loved one into God's hands and said, "God, she is yours." And you know it -- you leave her in God's hands and walk away strong because you are confident.

Or

You have received forgiveness because you confessed something deeply hidden. You have a sense of peace because you have been reconciled.

What are the experiences which enable you to say, "I think I have experienced God? I have come unto His truth and listened to His voice."

To be spiritually mature is to have a sense of your being and know who you are and what you are like.

To be spiritually mature is to be able to identify yourself with somebody and to sense that somebody is affirmed by God.

You are who you are because you have recognized that power -- a power beyond yourself who is saying "Yes to you, affirming you."

It isn't that God belongs to you -- you know you belong to God. Someone said, "The more I pray, the better it goes, and the less I pray, the worse it goes." If you have this sense in you, then you are maturing in the spirit. You are beginning to acknowledge the Truth that surrounds you.

The spiritual adult is always growing. This usually means being drawn into the lives of others. When he identifies with them in the spirit, he is there to strengthen them, support them. He never tries to remake them, judge them, reform them in His own image.

When the mature Christian trusts in the Spirit and the leading of the Spirit, he is open not only to life and people, but he is open to mystery.

The more he moves toward the mystery of all life in the Spirit, the more he can appropriate all the experiences of life -- the bad as well as the good -- and know that somehow in the Spirit they all make sense because they all make up the fabric of life.

To be able to trust that mystery, that truth, is to be spiritually mature. The key is the trusting of the Spirit each day, a day at a time. It is putting your trust in the process of living based on your own experience -- no one else's, only yours. You decide. It is your life.

Don't look to somebody else to straighten your life out. Don't lool to somebody else to give you the meaning of life. Don't look to somebody else to tell you how you should love. Don't look to somebody else to give the answers to the mystery of life. It is a mystery for everyone.

No one else can tell you, What's what.

Only He, the Savior, who came into the world. "And all who are not deaf to truth must listen to His voice."

What does mean something here is the Spirit you trust, the Spirit that comes to you, and dwells in you and guides your heart as you trust Him.

If you try to bend life, to make it your own, you distrust it. So treat it gently, love it, kiss it, then you will be carried by it into the glory of eternity. That is the Spirit -- living in Him. Now and always. That is the sense of joy for which all people seek.

The mystery that has baffled thoughtful, sensitive people from the beginning of time has been made clear for Christian people.

Not to be deaf to the truth, to listen to His voice -- that is the "Hope of Glory."

Given at St. Paul's Church in Bremerton, WA, November 25, 1979

Without Me

Without me, ye can do nothing. (John 15:5)

Commentary

Are you capable of doing things without any help? Can you resolve problems on your own? Do you question others' rationale for requesting assistance in a challenge? My Father preached about the attitude of people who claim they need no help, that they are entirely able to handle the situation on their own.

I understand these people. I have been one of them. I had an attitude of rebellious freedom from the mockery of being incapable of success at a simple task or job. I have endured the humiliation of failure because I did not accept assistance. I have amended my thinking to agree with the words of this sermon. We can do nothing without God's help.'

How about you, reading my commentary and then thinking I'm a lunatic for what I write and believe? Are you one of the "Can do" people who poopoo any recommended help? I swear, I understand from where you are coming.

I began my high school years 1700 miles away from home at Shattuck School (Shattuck/St. Mary's, today), a private residential, parochial military academy in the middle of Minnesota. An adventure was about to become a building of my independent streak of "Can do" without you. I began my three years of learning as a cadet private, newboy in the fall of 1964. I traveled from Portland, Oregon, on a train to Minneapolis, Minnesota, without any escort or idea what I was doing. I was a musician and was assigned to Band Company, First Platoon, Second squad. I played the trumpet but afterward I switched to a treble baritone and learned the instrument as best I could.

I drilled on the military field with the other members of the squad and platoon and company. Our senior and junior officers and sergeants trained us in the proper manner of marching. During military reviews, the Band Company played Sousa Marches and kept the Battalion in uniform step. My first year was a learning experience I will not forget, and I do not regret it. I was quite able to become a first-rate soldier all by myself.

By the time I was finished with Shattuck in June of 1967, I had attained the rank of First Lieutenant and command of Second Platoon, Band Company. My parents attended the graduation ceremonies, and I could tell they were proud parents. I had done a great achievement without anyone helping me other than the teaching staff, older students, and military personnel, which was their job. I was a success.

College at Oregon State University began in the Fall of 1967 and was not the same independent personal triumph I believed I had at Shattuck. When the year was finished, my educational success was less than stellar. I received a letter in the summer of 1968 stating I was not acceptable for a return for another year of schooling. Ouch.

Maybe I wasn't as independent as I wanted to be. I stayed with my parents in Longview, Washington, where Dad was the priest at St. Stephen's Episcopal Church. I applied for and was accepted to be a student at Lower Columbia College for my second year. My attitude had a significant shift from independent to "God, Help!"

I did manage to complete my college education in the required four years with a Bachelor of Arts in Education. God became a part of my life as I began a career teaching in Kitsap County. I attended St. Paul's Church and readily prayed for guidance from the Holy Spirit, Jesus Christ, and God.

Sermon

It sounds strange, doesn't it, to be told we can do nothing without God's help. We feel, both as individuals and as a nation, that we can do anything, and we plan our lives accordingly. Americans never seem to feel helpless. And yet, that is not Christian thinking, nor is it Christian teaching. Both the Bible and the Prayer Book bring out the idea that man continually needs God's help or grace of God.

Most of us never really believe the first article of the Creed. Most of us never really obey the First Commandment. We do not "put our confidence" -- for that is what "believe" means -- in One God who is almighty, and we do worship at least one other God besides the One True one. That means, of course, that we put our confidence in ourselves and prefer our own judgment to God's. This is what we call "Sin," obeying ourselves rather than God. It is just another name for selfishness.

But in the record of the Bible, whenever God calls a man to do something, He promises him His help. He said to Moses, "My presence shall go with thee, and I will give thee rest." (Exodus 33:14) The Psalmist is always asking God for help and always being thankful for what God has done for his soul.

Praise the Lord, O my soul, and forget not all His benefits. (Psalm 103:2) And the Prayer Book, which gives us collects or little prayers to be said in common with others when we come to church or in our private devotions, is true to the Bible teaching.

The collect for this Sunday, the 19th after Trinity, says, "O God, for as much as without thee we are not able to please thee." Again, in the collect for the first Sunday after Trinity: "O God, the strength of all those who put their trust in thee: mercifully accept our prayers; and because, through the weakness of our mortal nature, we can do no good thing without thee; grant us the help of thy grace." That little prayer gives the reason, "Through the weakness of our mortal nature." We are like the poor man in the Parable of the Good Samaritan; we are "half-dead," and we need help.

When a man knows that he needs help, or God's grace -- that is what "grace" means, "God's help" -- then God can help him and is ready to help him. Did you ever read the Fifty-first Psalm to yourself? The Psalm we read on Ash Wednesday in Church. The writer of the Psalm really "came to himself." He knew he was "half dead." He knew that it was only God who could help him and who could save him. That was why he poured out his heart in words that devout Jews and devout Christians have used for centuries. When we realize our need, our own helplessness, then is the time that we find God. For God does not work with proud souls: "God resisteth the proud, but giveth grace unto the humble." (James 4:6) And God does give grace.

Where does God give grace? God gives grace in and through the church. First, there is the grace or help he gives at Baptism. You remember that answer from the Catechism to the question if we thought we ought to keep our Baptismal vows? "Yes, verily," we say, "and by God's help, so I will." And I heartily thank our heavenly Father, that he hath called me to this state of salvation through Jesus Christ, our Savior. And I pray unto God to give me his grace, that I may continue in the same unto my life's end. Hold fast to this Baptismal grace. And then in the Holy Communion, God gives us grace or help "for the continual strengthening and refreshing" our souls -- words from the Catechism again. There is also the Church's book, the Bible or Holy Scriptures. In it, we see how God has dealt with other people just like us. He called them. He led them. He corrected them -- His rod and His staff comforted them -- but He helped them. He helped them when they realize their helplessness, and He helped them again and again and again...

Furthermore, The Church teaches us to pray. That is, it gives us the words to use, the vocabulary of Prayer, and when to use them. Prayer is not merely asking God's help for ourselves. It is confessing or telling God we have disobeyed, neglected, or forgotten Him. It is thanking Him for all He has done for us and others. It is adoration or telling Him we love Him. Prayer is learning to know God and learning to know His will for us. If we talk with a person, we find out what that person is like, and we find out also what he likes and does not like. Talking with God gives the same results. We find out what He is like, and we also find out what He likes us to do to please Him and what He does not want us to do.

You have heard the expression "getting right with God." That is what we mean when we say a man has to realize he is helpless and needs God's help or grace. The correct name for that condition is Humility. Humility is not an inferiority complex. It does not mean that we are not good that we cannot do anything or amount to anything. Humility realizes our need for God's help. A humble man knows what he can do, but he also knows what he cannot do. So we can say that a Christian never feels forsaken. For a Christain knows that God is with him. Our Lord said to St. Paul, "My grace is sufficient for thee." (IICor 12:9) St. Paul was a truly humble man. you remember he said, "Not that we are sufficient of ourselves -- but our sufficiency is of God." He always realized he had to have God's help for the task of converting the Gentiles.

When the mother of James and Jon asked our Lord if her two sons might sit on His right hand and on His left in the Kingdom, He turned to them said, "Are you able?" He wanted them as He wants us to realize we can do nothing without Him. "Without me, you can do nothing."

"I am the vine; ye are the branches: He that abideth in me, and I in him, the same bringeth forth much fruit; for without me ye can do nothing." (John 15:5) This verse is just another way of saying that the Church is the body of Christ, and all baptized people the members. We are grafted on to the true Vine at our Baptism, and the life from that true Vine flows through us. That is why St. Paul could say, "I can do all things through Christ who strengthens me." (Phil 4:13) And that is why a Christian never really feels helpless nor forsaken. Like the Canaanite woman, we say, "Lord, help me."
Like the Psalmist, we say, "I will go forth in the strength of the Lord, God." That is a good prayer to say when we leave our room in the morning, "I will go forth in the strength of the Lord, God."

Our great saint said, "Prayer is the loving attention upon God." If we wait or attend on God, the results will be this: we shall always realize that without Him, we cannot please him, but we shall want to please Him. And when we want to please Him, then His Holy Spirit will in all things direct and rule our hearts.

Given at St. Mark's, Moscow and Palouse, Idaho, June 21, 1953
Church of the Ascension, Twin Falls, Idaho, May 22, 1955
North Adams, Massachusetts, July 3, 1955
Church of the Ascension, Twin Falls, Idaho, July 7, 1957

Jesus Dispirited

This is more than we can stomach! Why listen to such talk.
(John 6:60)

Commentary

What compels a person to continue pursuing a dream while all the people around them are reluctant to listen? As a teacher for over thirty years, I encountered students who flourished in class with my guidance and other students who floundered. The ones most frustrating were pupils who did not want to participate. They listened, thought about the lesson, and gave up.

Jesus must have had similar experiences. At times, I asked my reluctant students the same type of question Jesus asked. "Do you want another teacher?" We all become disenchanted by others' 'actions when the unexpected occurs. I have encountered similar feelings with my children.

We are a close family now and share time together when we can. Sandy and I provide childcare, we dine together, travel to the beaches and mountains of Washington, and outings to sporting events. Could Jesus have predicted the reluctance of people to decipher His words? Could He have better communicated in a way to encourage them? I don't know.

This sermon addresses issues I think still exist. We are a nation of wealth and prosperity. Yet, we are determined not to do what is asked of us by Jesus Christ. Many of us are selfish, egocentric, power-hungry, and greedy. We want signs from Christ that prove His worthiness as a leader. We ask the same of our leaders. Where has that gotten us?

Deeds are not an answer to our questions, but they guide what we believe and want. We act according to our faith in a situation or a set of conditions. We are quick to jump on the bandwagon of the next idol of social media. The actions of some convince us that their way is the right way. Consequences be damned.

I'm sure Jesus faced much of the same controversy in His lifetime. Had He been able to convince the Hebrew leaders that He was indeed the Son of God, life would be very different today. Maybe our guilty minds are reacting in a way to hide our assumed failure to follow Jesus. We are not interested in understanding His words when they conflict with what we extoll as our desires.

As far as today is concerned, demonstrations and marches to seek social and legal justice can provide a cathartic moment for humans to reflect on actions that controvert the teachings of Jesus. We can modify our lives to benefit from what we are pursuing for our betterment. We are free to be who we want to be.

However we live, we are subject to our failures to attract people to a message that can ensure a paradise on Earth and eternal life in Heaven. Jesus asked His disciples if they would leave Him, and Peter responded with an answer we all need to hear. "To whom shall we go? Your words are eternal life." I'm prepared to listen and learn life lessons from the one true and everlasting person who's spirit does not waver even when He asks if we are to leave as others have done.

Sermon

Jesus had just given a discourse on Himself as the Bread of Life. In Him was life eternal. The people couldn't understand or stomach his teaching. They deserted Him right and left. The same happens today.

He said, "The words which I have spoken to you are both spirit and life." And yet there are of some you who have no faith. Many of His disciples withdrew and were no longer with Him. So Jesus asked the twelve. "Do you also want to leave me?"

Peter answered, "Lord, to whom shall we go? Your words are words of eternal life."

In Robert Browning's Easter Day poem, he writes, "How very hard it is to be a Christian." Jesus Christ could not tone down the faith and make it easier for us by emasculating it.

Constantly, unswerving, He stood by His truth that the deep facts and doctrines must be preached whether the people liked it or not, whether they alienated or attracted, whether folks thronged to hear or would not listen. And He did preach to them at the cost of losing many of His followers.

We read in the Gospels that wherever Jesus went, He was surrounded by great crowds. At Capernaum, "All the city was gathered together at the door." Five thousand gathered when He fed them.

For three years, Jesus did nothing else than go about teaching and healing. And if ever a person had these capacities which command his message and person to others, it was Jesus of Nazareth.

He was a superb teacher. His parables, sermon, and teachings have never been surpassed. He taught with such compassion and understanding that he reached religious leaders, fishermen, wealthy aristocrats, peasants, Jews, Samaritans, Greeks, and Romans.

He was the greatest healer ever known to man. More than this, He had what no other had so fully: the example of His own life. Everything thus taught was in His life before it was in His words.

So here is a person who gave three years of His life to the work of making Christians, gifted with all the qualities that were personal loyalty. The results should have been stupendous.

They were -- At the end of His ministry, He was betrayed by one of His closest disciples, illegally tried, hastily condemned, and brutally killed, which is precisely what He predicted would happen.

In the book of Acts, we are told that after Christ was put to death, the number of followers was only one hundred twenty. Considering all things, the founder of our faith did not do a very good job of making Christians. It was evident well before the end that His methods were not achieving great success.

As the Gospel story tells us this morning, He was being deserted so rapidly that He asked His immediate disciples if they were also leaving.

He had been given several suggestions that might have helped make Him popular. Make free food for all believers by turning stones into bread. He could pull off some spectacular stunt. He could raise an army of patriots and malcontents. Or He could go into hiding. But He seemed to have the idea that the only way to do what He was trying to do was the way He was doing it.

First of all, He was calling all people to repentance. Change their motivations and actions. He stressed what He called the inner ethic priority of nature. Good trees bring forth good fruit. His call to men was to reconcile to the God of Life.

Christians today have been subjected to quite a barrage of criticism for their alleged failure to make the world Christian. We have been taunted with loving a religion of escapism, ivory-towered isolationism, and selfishness.

We know our reputation is incomplete, our ethic imperfect of devotion to the Love of God, lukewarm. Making Christians was not easy in Christ's earthly lifetime. Making Christians today is not easy.

Today every honest attempt to make people Christian runs into the same difficulties as our Lord faced. People cannot be forced into repentance. They cannot be driven to righteousness. They cannot be compelled to recognize Jesus as the Son of God.

The only force we can use is the force of love. We can teach, we can love it, and with the help of God, we can take the consequences. That is what our Lord expected Himself and what He told us to expect.

It is high time that we get over our feelings of guilt that we have failed to make everybody Christian. Our Lord couldn't succeed, and we can't either. After we have repented for our ignorance, sin, and lack of devotion; after we have recognized that we have neither the understanding, the courage, nor the love so evident in Our Savior, the fact remains; so long as we have His purposes and use His methods, and are loyal to Him, we are going to achieve the same results He did. Making Christians is not easy.

Given at St. Paul's Church, Bremerton, WA,
September 2, 1976 and August 26, 1979

Not servants ... Friends

Henceforth I call you not servants; -- but I have called you friends; -- You have not chosen me, but I have chosen you and ordained you.
(John 15:15-16)

Commentary

Many of us have friends, and we share our time with them. Some friends are closer in proximity while others are at a distance and connected by the internet. I enjoy my friends, but the pandemic we experienced in 2020 crimped our connections but not our spirit. With the words John attributes to Jesus, we learn that Jesus was interested in being friends with His disciples.

All of us are called to servitude in one way or another by providing for family and church. We are employed in occupations that service companies and clients. We are in manufacturing and sales, providing the goods a host of people desire and want. We sate human desires with continued service to jobs and occupations.

However, we are not servants or slaves or chattel. Jesus asked us to perform services to people as part of our faith in His teachings. We call upon the skills we possess to provide those services. But Jesus was not interested in Servants as much as He wanted friends who served. Service was not a direct requirement for faith, but without it, are we truly faithful?

In this twenty-first century of COVID-19 pandemic and an economic recession or depression, Christians are called to servanthood and selflessness in giving of our talents to others in need. Jesus has called us to be friends with those we do not know and share with those who are not friends. We are asked to deliver needed services and goods to others for our survival during this crisis.

How is it that we are unaware of the attributes of being friends and not servants? Why do we balk at the concept of helping others and weighing the consequences of selfishness and self-righteousness? Can we be ordained by Jesus as His disciples and ignore other's plights in today's dilemmas?

Friends are found in strange places. The internet abounds with people whom we friend on Facebook or follow on Instagram. The news is rife with stories of people rallying to aid others in crisis because of the death of men and women at the hands of over-zealous police officers or anarchists wanting the government's destruction. We should listen to the plights of others and act as servants who are friends. Jesus wants our friendship as we provide the service He asks of us.

While you read my father's sermon contemplate how loving another human being, without regard for ethnicity, color, creed, gender, or gender-identification, sexual preferences, or any of the myriad biases placed in our way to befriending another person, leads us to Jesus Christ and discovering the love God possesses for His universal creation. We are tasked to succeed when all others fail. Let us go forth and love one another as Jesus loved us in the sacrament of His body and blood.

Sermon

This past week your rector visited a family, the mother of which was the only Episcopalian. To his surprise and delight, for over an hour, they asked one question after another concerning the doctrines, ministry, history, and customs of the Episcopal Church. They even asked why some of the clergy wore black suits and some gray and how much one was supposed to put in the plate when passed. At the end of the hour, the parents, who had apologized for asking so many questions, said they were determined to send their children to Church School and to enter the fellowship of the Church.

Undoubtedly there are thousands of families in this country who know very little about the Episcopal Church and are reluctant to ask questions that display their ignorance. Many of them would become active members if only it were possible to answer the questions that are in their minds. Let us today think especially concerning the

Church and the ministry, taking as our text the words of our Lord: "Henceforth I call you not servants; -- but I have called you friends; -- ye have not chosen me, but I have chosen you." These were Jesus' solemn but moving words to those men He had especially called and ordained to found the Holy Catholic Church of which we are now members.

During the Advent season the Church calls us to remember St. John the Baptist, the last of the prophets, and the first to proclaim Jesus as the lamb of God. He was called the Forerunner of the Lord, the one who went before to announce his coming. In a true sense, all ministers of Christ's Church are His forerunners, who proclaim His coming now and on the day of Judgement. With this in mind, let us consider briefly the Gospel today, the Church in these times, and the Christian ministry.

First, then, what is the Gospel today? Is it just morality touched with emotion, the good life with plenty of kindly deeds? Is it merely a philosophy embroidered with mystic phrases? Or just the fascinating story of a good man's life and death?

We believe that the Gospel is the great revelation of the out-reaching love of God through Jesus Christ as Savior and Friend of all. We understand it to be a call to high fellowship with the Infinite God, through Him, who said, "Henceforth, I call you not servants; -- but I have called you friends." Now and then, some people will say that we need a new religion for these troubled times. But to us, the Gospel is no human creation to be cast aside for some new light. It reveals for all time the character and love of God through His son, Jesus Christ.

What then, is the Church of Christ? If H. G. Wells was right when he said, "Jesus Christ is easily the dominant figure of all history;" if He is in fact "The Holiest among the mighty and the mightiest among the holy," as Fairbairn said; then we shall expect to find His church no small proposition. From the very beginning, the Church has been criticized, persecuted, and attacked with loud voices ever proclaiming its failure and approaching downfall. Yet who can deny that this Church has shown amazing survival power? Who can gainsay the fact that it is today the oldest and strongest organization in the world? The Church's Book, the Holy Bible, has been for generations the world's best-seller, and you may be sure that as many people go to church today as ever wanted to. The Christian can still sing:

"Oh where are kings and empires now,
    Of old, that went and came?
But, Lord, thy Church is praying yet,
    A thousand years the same."

When we hear someone indulging in the favorite sport of knocking the Church and expressing what is wrong with the clergy, it is well to remember such criticism is a real tribute to the institution's power. The very existence of the Church is a standing challenge to those whose lives run contrary to the Gospel. Many of those critics, whose voices are loudest against religion and the church, are really telling the world that their consciences are troubled by the sound of bells calling to worship and the sight of multitudes receiving strength and light from worship. Every clergyman knows that he can hardly walk down the street without meeting someone who sees his round collar and feels moved to defend himself for not coming to church.

Yes, the Church is ever the same and always a standing challenge for those who fail to follow the Lord Jesus. Yet, in another sense, the Church is ever-changing, ever meeting new conditions with new ways. It is the same old Gospel but expressed through new methods for a new generation. Some people are always lamenting that the Church is not what it used to be, imagining a sort of golden age of the past.

An old farmer once said to another, "Si ain't the same man he used to be."

"No," said his friend, "he never was." The Church, as the "blessed company of all faithful people," has always been human as well as divine. Never was that Church all that it might be. Of course, there are hypocrites in the pews and now and then at the altar and in the pulpit. But the Church has no monopoly on that pest. Where will you find any place or any organization without a few unworthy ones? If you expect to move out of any place where hypocrites are to be found, you will have to move off the face of the Earth.

Yet the Church with all its failings and divisions is undoubtedly, as Dr. Ernest allen has said, "far and away the greatest force for righteousness in the world today." Whenever you want any great and good undertaking put through, you must go, not to the irreligious and non-church population, but to your Church members who are in every community in the land the leaders in patriotism, charity, and idealism of every kind. No wonder Will Hays once said that religion was "the one essential industry in the United States."

What shall we then say of the ministry of the Church? How easy it is to make fun of a parson's blunders. How often people expect their paster to be a paragon of virtue, the learned scholar, the eloquent orator, the business executive, the skillful teacher of the young, the wise counselor of the aged, the hail-fellow-well-met, the devout man of God. But the most important thing about the ministry is that they are ambassadors of Christ, called, chosen, ordained by Him who said, Ye have not chosen me; -- but I have chosen you, and ordained you."

Some years ago, a certain man was chosen ambassador to a foreign country, and friends came to congratulate him. One said, " well, John, what a jolly time you'll have, hobnobbing with rulers. It must be great."

"Yes," replied the ambassador, "it is a great and tremendous thing to represent one's country." Let us never forget, then, that it is a great and tremendous thing to be called of God, not merely to be a leader in this business of keeping the soul of the world alive, but to be the living, personal representative of Jesus Christ, an ambassador of the Kingdom of Heaven.

Is it any wonder that from the earliest times, the ministry of bishops, priests, and deacons has been preserved as the historical, practical, and best way of accrediting and ordaining men for this sacred office? The three great historical branches of the Holy Catholic Church -- the Eastern Orthodox, the Roman Catholic, and our own Anglican Communion -- have carefully preserved this historical ministry. No man had been permitted to call himself an accredited ambassador without proper credentials of ordination by Christ. The various denominations, from Reformation times to the present, have done noble work, and no one can deny their membership in the universal Church. But it is a fact of history that most of them have lost the historic ministry of bishops, priests, and deacons, the apostolic laying-on-of-hands in Confirmation, and other things that we regard as valuable or essential. Some, like Mary Baker Eddys followers, have gone so far as to abolish Baptism and the Holy Communion.

    Not long ago, a man asked a certain rector if the church was not generally considered a failure. "Yes, and no, " replied the rector.

    "Why, what do you mean?" asked the man.

    "Well, the church is a failure,770 and so are the clergy as far as reaching the ideal, doing all they ought to do, making this world what it ought to be. But the Church is a tremendous success as the only organization exalting the worship of the one God, proclaiming the universal Christian Gospel, laboring for peace and justice, education and brotherhood." Yes, most certainly it has been a tremendous success.

We beseech Thee, Oh Lord, to guide Thy Church with Thy perpetual governance, that it may walk warily in times of quiet and boldly in times of trouble; through our Lord Jesus Christ. Amen

When this sermon was given is not recorded and therefore unknown.

Death and Resurrection

Now Bethany was less than two miles from Jerusalem, and many Jews had come to Martha and Mary to comfort them in the loss of their brother. When Martha heard that Jesus was coming, she went out to meet him, but Mary stayed at home. "LORD," Martha said to Jesus, "if you had been here, my brother would not have died. But I know that even now God will give you whatever you ask." Jesus said to her, "Your brother will rise again." Martha answered, "I know he will rise again in the resurrection at the last day." Jesus said to her, "I am the resurrection and the life. The one who believes in me will live, even though they die; (John 11:18-25)

Commentary

We all die at some point along our timeline. Whether we feel the end of living comes at the right moment or not, we are stuck with the knowledge we will die. Are we ready to accept the end without fear? I like to think my life will end at the appropriate moment in my lifeline and that I will have accomplished all that I have to do. I will set my son in a situation for his care to be covered. I will see my grandchildren grow to adulthood and success. I will write enough books to be known in the literary world. I will have helped my church family.

The challenge for us all is to accept that life will not care about our plans. The current crisis in health environs is the COVID-19 pandemic sweeping through our country without considering how we humans feel. The disease spreads without barriers as we try to continue living our healthy lives.

As of this writing, I am not exposed to the virus. At least I tell myself that I am free from infection. I must be careful as my wife is more vulnerable to the disease's effects than I may be. Her immune system does not work as well as it should to suppress and control the virus. So I take precautions of masking when out in the public arena. I use sanitation wipes and liquids to clear my hands of any viruses. I keep all of the goods I procure away from my wife, so she is not exposed to any germs that might live on the package surfaces.

But what happens when we die? I watched my father in 1986 and 1987 for ten months after a stroke as he slowly withered away. I was present five years ago as my mother, when diagnosed with cancer at 96 years of age, decided to forgo any treatment and died a couple of months later. I did not beg Jesus to come and save them. I waited for their life to ebb and end. I was not mournful at the end, as I believe in life after death and resurrection.

What happens after death is based on such stories as Martha and Mary believing their brother would live again in the resurrection. I developed my ideas on the writings in the Gospels about Jesus rising from death after three days.

I think about life's meaning and the millions and billions of people who lived before me. They had their timeline to follow as do I. We are necessarily locked into a mystery for which we have only Jesus Christ explaining what is next.

Are we capable of resurrection? Do we understand it? Can we endure the process? I don't know the answers to any of these queries. But like Mary, I trust in Jesus fulfilling our next experiences living again in this world or the next, resurrected in mind or body or both and with our souls intact. Read what my father had to say to his congregation nearly 50 years ago.

Sermon

Sometimes our worldly wisdom and human experiences belie some of the great truths of life. The longer I live and study God's word, the more I realize that the central and most fundamental truths of Jesus, which have brought new hope and courage to human souls, were given in the first place to single, seemingly unimportant individuals. People such as the woman at the well of Sacher, the man born blind or Nicodemus. Today's Gospel is about Martha in her hour of sorrow.

Our admiration for Martha grows as we think of her quietness, self-restraint, strength of mind and faith, and character. Obviously, she had been hoping against hope that an answer to her prayer, Christ would come in time to help Lazarus.

But there is not a whisper of reproach over his failure to appear. Only that sad, heart-gripping, wistful: "Lord, if you had been here., my brother would not have died."

If-If-If

But it was not to be. Martha says, "And even now I know that whatever you ask of God, God will give you."

What did she mean by that? Probably she herself hardly knew. Yet for those who know Christ at all well, like Martha, they come to Him in a blind trust.

They do not know what He will feel is right to do, or what they might ask from Him. But they are entirely sure of his interest in them, His compassion toward them, and His power to carry through for good. And they leave it at that with quiet and contented minds.

And is it not our extraordinary tribute to Christ and His love where we leave our beloved dead so confidently in His keeping? We have loved them so much and know so little of that other world to which they have gone. And yet we let them go without fear. Why?

Because Jesus is there. They are His. He will not forget them. Whatever he asked for them, God will give them.

Such is the faith of those who know Christ and commit their loved one to Him.

"Your brother will rise again," said Jesus.

To which Martha answers bravely, "I know that he will rise again in the resurrection on the last day." And that his the faith which transforms these human lives of ours and puts new sense and meaning and depth and glory in them.

So Christ gave to Martha that great truth which has been recited at innumeralable funerals into poor souls stunned and agonized. Hearing it, their hearts are softened, and their faith renewed.

"I am the resurrection and the life. He who believes in me, though he were dead, yet shall he live and whoever lives and believes in me shall never die."

But also, as Christ said. "This is for the living and not for the dead." So in this present life, Christ has been for untold multitudes the resurrection and the life.

Through Christ and in Him, in this world, people who have been half dead, become alive, grow sensitive, active, and purposeful, empowered with powers they did not have before.

This is a claim of absolute truth. The Apostles Creed Evangelists were sure of it. People in all times have staked their lives on it.

And St. Paul, in that magnificent passage of Ephesians, says, "And you, He made alive, where you were dead through trespasses and sins in which you once worked, ... But God, who is rich in mercy, out of the great love with which He loved us, even when we were dead through our trespasses, made us alive together with Christ.

In this sense, it has been proved over and over again that "he who believes in me, though he were dead, yet shall he live."

You can explain it any way you like -- but this has happened over and over again. And the only possible solution is Christ.

When men believe in Him, this happens. Without Him, it does not.

But Jesus was speaking to a woman whose brother was dead, and whose heart was sore and broken. And what He said leaped out across the barriers of death, giving us a tremendous promise for future life.

"Whosoever believes in me shall never die."

"Do you believe this," Christ asked Martha.

And bravely, she answered that she did. Yet her understanding of it all was at best dim and cloudy. So is ours.

And yet what a difference it makes to us to hold this faith, however weak -- to dare to credit God's strange love for us, and the salvation he has wrought for us in Christ.

And that in Him, our dreams are not only dreams but truths of what one day will really be.

Give at St. Paul's Churh, Bremerton, WA., July 15, 1973

Mary and Martha

When Martha heard that Jesus was coming, she went out to meet him, but Mary stayed at home. (John 11:20)

Commentary

The story of Martha and Mary is a sad tale of family heartache because of death. All humanity faces the loss of brothers and sisters, parents, and grandparents. The closer we are emotionally to these people, the harder it is to accept the death and continue with life. I witnessed my Dad's stroke and subsequent death after ten months of caring for him with my mother. I experienced my mother's diagnosis of cancer at age 96, and her death two months later. Neither death was dramatic nor heart-wrenching. They had lived long lives and produced three capable children, adults with families of their own.

Susan, John, and I are proud parents and grandparents. We enjoy our families and spend time with them often. Unlike Martha and Mary, we have not endured losing a brother or a sister. We are alive and healthy. We are now 76, 71, and 68. We have not lost any of our children or grandchildren to disease or accidents. What we have that keeps us together as a family is the same fundamental power that Martha and Mary had. Faith.

During the COVID-19 pandemic raging throughout the world, as I write this commentary, in July of 2020 many people have experienced a loss of family members to the virus. Some are children. Some are young adults. Some are close to other family members, which causes significant pain. Most are older members of the family who have lived full lives. The emptiness remains, though, and each of the individuals who feel the loss must figure out how to continue living.

The Good news in my father's sermon is that Jesus preached to us about what is expected from us as followers of his teachings. We are called to know that His love is sufficient. That each of us will be better for accepting His love and knowing it is without conditions.

Can we as followers love each other unconditionally in a faith that presses us to accept the object of something based on evidence but without infallible truth. Are we capable of taking the risk that someone we do not know has a plan for us? Will we put in a proper effort to support our faith? What we want in this corporeal world may not have the trust of knowing the real Jesus Christ. We will have to be faithful to a commitment that places people together in following Jesus in a way that He showed us by loving us unconditionally.

Sermon

The controversy of Mary and Martha is ageless. There are those like Martha who argue that the merits of a job well done, and the business of life is all that matters.

And there are those like Mary who derive their strength and insight from Prayer, Meditation and being with the Lord. It isn't a matter of either/or but both areas.

Let me tell you a tale I heard from Keith Miller years ago, which illustrates some of the differences in belief as an intellectual exercise and a living experiment. This letter was found in a baking powder can wired to the handle of an old pump that offered the only hope of drinking water on a very long and seldom-used trail across Death Valley.

It said, "This pump is all right as of June 1932. I put a new sucker washer in it, and it might last for years. But the washer dries out, and the pump has got to be primed. I buried a bottle of water, out of the sun, and cork end up. There's enough water in it to prime the pump, but not if you drink some first. Pour about one fourth and let her soak to wet the leather. Then pour in the rest medium fast and pump like crazy. You'll git water. The well has never run dry. Have faith. When you git water, fill up the bottle and put it back like you found it for the next feller." (signed) Desert Pete. "P.S., Don't go drinking up the water first. Prime the pump with it, and you'll git all you can hold."

Here is an illustration of faith and work in action. As reflected in the story, faith is composed of three ingredients. First, there must be an object. It is impossible just "to have faith." If you were a lonely, parched traveler in that desert, you would have to trust an unknown person named Desert Pete to keep from drinking the bottle of buried water. This would not be easy. He is a person you do not know. There is no guarantee that he is not a practical joker or a lunatic. So the first ingredient of faith is trust in someone or something based on evidence but not infallible truth.

The second ingredient is Risk. Faith is always costly. Desert Pete tells you that if you drink any part of the bottle of water he has left, you won't get any from the pump. So it seems necessary to risk the very stuff on which your life may depend to get a safe and sufficient amount. Faith is always expressive.

The third ingredient is Work. Some people have mistakenly interpreted faith as a substitute for work. Faith is not laziness. Desert Pete reminds us that after faith and risk, we have to pump like crazy.

So much for faith in general, But what about Christian faith? The ingredients are the same. First of all, you have to have faith in God, especially in the way God has revealed himself to humanity in the person of Jesus Christ. It is not faith in a principle but faith in a Person. Thee Person.

Second, there is a commitment that involves Risk. Total commitment means asking forgiveness of another, making specific restitution, beginning to tithe, or changing jobs, or lifestyle. The more we commit ourselves to God in specific ways, the better we can know Him and His plan for our lives.

Third, there is hard work. Some people have interpreted the X in faith as just a matter of hard work. This leads to a kind of living which may be religious, but it is not Christian. Christian faith is more than hard work for Christ and His Kingdom. I have never known an effective, dedicated Christain who was lazy.

In the New Testament, we read about the call to commitment, which Jesus extended to the first disciple. It was a person to person call. They were not called to believe in a doctrine, practice ethics, or worship in a prescribed way. They were called to trust Jesus and follow Him.

The call was not to people who could be considered spiritual types, those who naturally enjoy prayer, meditation, and the esthetics of work. Instead, Jesus called people who were virile, earthy, and ordinary. Jesus is no respecter of persons. Men, women, and young people from every walk of life who are willing to respond are called.

In the New Testament, the message seems clear that the new life offered by Jesus Christ begins when we repent and believe. Repentance is the time of "coming to one's self."

And belief for the Christian is not an intellectual exercise but rather a call to experience belief, or faith, meaning turning to God as He is revealed in Jesus Christ and testing his love and nature.

A right relationship means one has heard the good news that God says to us in Jesus Christ. "I love you." I love you as you are. I love you, unconditionally. And now, all I ask is that you begin to respond to my love and commitment to you by committing to me all of yourself you are able to give.

If this is what the Cross is all about, if this is what Jesus Christ has accomplished by His Incarnation and Atonement, then we are talking about Good News that is almost too good to be true.

Given at St. Paul's Church, Bremerton, WA, October 17, 1977

Who is Jesus Christ?

"Look," John said, "there is the Lamb of God. It is He who takes away the sin of the world." (John 1:29)

Commentary

For centuries people across the globe have asked this one fundamental question. Was he a real person? Did he teach lessons and provide examples that describe the tenets of belief for Christians today? What was His life like in Judea and Galilee?

The writings of the Gospels relate the life and times of Jesus Christ in vivid detail. As with any essays, those of us in this present time might question the validity of the narrative. Overall, though, I think the stories are accurate accountings by people who lived in the same place at the same time as Jesus.

I studied history and social sciences as a student in college. Reading the accounts of various writers who researched people's writings about the life of Jesus can make a person skeptical. Enough variation of source materials with a commonality of information helps develop the reliability of the historical record. We accept some information as trustworthy and question other information when it seems outlandish.

Was Jesus an outlandish character in the imagination of the Gospel writers? Does enough material exist to support the claims purported in the Bible stories? I want to believe and have faith in the words they wrote. Although they did not experience Jesus first hand, they did meet the people who knew Jesus. I accept the writings because scholarly reviews have authenticated the original manuscripts.

Now then, we need to know Jesus, and my father's sermon addresses the idea of who he was and is. We are in a faith-building mode as we learn more about the man whose life shook the foundations of Judaism to the point of executing an innocent man for teaching alternative lessons of God's words.

We have more knowledge of the solar system and our galaxy than the people two thousand years ago. We have unlocked the secrets of the universe so that we know the pins of light in the sky are actually other stars and galaxies. We have traveled to the moon and back. We have sent probes out to other planets.

And yet, we are skeptical of a man who lived and died two thousand years ago. The teaching of this man had a profound impact on the world. They have reached billions of people who believe. So, who is Jesus? Read what my father preached and discover if any of the mystery makes sense.

Sermon

In the Gospel story related to us by John 1: 29-41, "Look," John said, "there is the Lamb of God. It is He who takes away the sins of the world."

"This is God's chosen one."

Andrew said to Peter, "We have found the Messiah."

For 2000 years, people of Jesus Christ have been saying these same things. At our worship, we stand together and say, "I believe in Jesus Christ."

As Jesus asked long ago, "Who do people say that I am?"

And the answer from the disciples, "That you are the living Christ - the Son of God." What does this mean for you and me? Who is this person that you and I worship and try to open our lives to?

To some impatient souls, all this may seem quite theoretical and highly speculative. What's the good of all the subtle distinctions anyway? The point is that faith and practice go together. And a wholesome Christian life is the fruit of sound Christian faith. What we think of Christ is truly important.

For practical purposes, let us approach the question of the deity of our Lord from four different angles. First is His own human life, that calls for an explanation because of its superlative difference from any other life that has ever lived. His sinlessness, His loyalty, His compassion, His assurance, His insight into human nature, His grasp of eternal values are all beyond natural imagination. His matchless teaching and His example of that teaching are without parallel. In all the records of human history, His life stands unique.

Second is what He thought of Himself. On His authority, He set aside requirements for the Law which to the Jews were of divine origin, and he supplanted them with His commandments. He accepted worship and adoration from His followers. He identified Himself with the Heavenly Father -- "I and my Father are one.?" No man knoweth the Son, but the Father; neither knoweth any man the Father, save the Son, and he whomsoever the Son will reveal him."

Peter said, "Thou art the Christ." at this time of His trial, the High Priest placed Him under oath and demanded, "Art thou the Christ?"

Jesus replied, "I am." There was no doubt about what He meant, for His accused took him to trial, saying, "He makes Himself equal to God." The records are full of it. There can only be three answers;

1) He was a fraud.
2) He was deluded.
3) He spoke the truth.

For all Christians down through the ages, we believe He spoke the truth.

Third is what others thought of Him. "I believe that Jesus Christ is the son of God," said the Ethiopian, who had been prepared for baptism. St. Peter repeatedly speaks of "The Lord and Savior, Jesus Christ."

St. John wrote, "Whoso shall confess that Jesus is the Son of God, God dwelleth in Him." All the early Christians were Jews. For them to attribute divine power to other than the God of their Fathers would have been a reversal of all their training unless they were convinced of the absolute truth. They staked their lives on their faith.

Fourth is the Christian experience. The Christian community worshipped Christ as God from the beginning. In every age, the best minds have worshipped and adored Him while the common people have given their lives to Him. Countless lives have been revolutionized by faith in His divine mission. He has affected society the whole world over.

What this means to you and me is that God's love and mercy are no longer academic qualities. He has lived our lives and face our troubles. God knows and understands because He has been here, too. When we approach God, we come to a friend and companion who has struggled with life as we know it. It is a better world to live in because God became incarnate in Jesus Christ, our Lord.

One last note: our Christian faith is always progressive. It looks not to the past but into the future. We do not reverence a dead hero. Instead, we worship a living Lord. Christ is not back yonder -- He is up ahead -- leading the way.

Given at St. Paul's Church, Bremerton, WA on January 1, 1972.

Negativism to Positivism

"This beginning of miracles did Jesus in Cana of Galilee, and manifested forth his glory, and his disciples believed on him."
John 2:11

Commentary

Earlier in this book, I commented on the same story of changing water into wine at a wedding in Cana. My focus in that earlier narrative was on the miracle and the stake it had on the ministry of Jesus. The wedding was a blessing, and running out of wine was a travesty averted when Jesus asked that jars be filled with water and then be tested for the fineness of the wine.

This sermon focuses on another aspect of the event. We are subject to the same trials and tribulations of our frail lives as those attending the wedding. We plan as best we can and still are subjected to failure. Embarrassment can do irreparable harm to psyches and street credibilities. A person can wallow in despair on the negative results of actions or lack of actions and squander valuable energy and time.

At the time of this commentary the world is experiencing negative activities and behaviors by many disgruntled people. In the United States, the Black Lives Matter movement has focused on the adverse history of race relations. Confederate monuments and flags are being displaced or removed from prominence in the southern states that seceded in 1861 leading to a devastating war that killed over 5% of the male population in four years.

The results of the relations between whites and blacks have continued negatively since those days. Many citizens committed to change attitudes and laws. With a national presidential election this November, politicians are listening and proposing changes to sway public opinion that they are on the right side of the issues.

The other negative in the world is the COVID-19 pandemic raising havoc in many countries of the world. The United States leads the nations in the number of cases and deaths. Political scandal and negative behaviors have been attributed to leaders' seemingly callous attitude in some parts of this country. As more cases arise in hotspot areas and deaths continue an upward trend, citizens demand more action by government leaders.

How do these negatives relate to positivism? As my father stated in his sermon, Jews lived meticulous lives by the law. As a result, they subjected themselves to minimalism. They did the least act to comply with the requirements. Many people today want the minimum requirements and then to be left alone to do as they wish. This attitude has not provided a resolution to the issues of race and economic disparity nor the conquering of the ravages of coronavirus outbreaks in the world.

God created a simple process for making water into wine. We need a simple process to change attitudes about our fellow citizens and the differences in race, creed, color, ethnicity, gender identification, and sexual preferences. We should act in a simple, positive manner to change our water into wine as quickly as Jesus did at the wedding in Cana. If only we knew how to make the changes without having to follow a lengthy method of demonstrations and marches regarding social relationships. If only we had a quick process to make an antiviral vaccination. Can Jesus provide the proper adjustments to the current infectious situation? Possibly, but we all need to be and act in a positive way.

What is the positive way? I wish I had an answer that fits each person on this planet. I don't have such insight. Jesus Christ had this insight and preached the truth to anyone who wanted to hear. So many people did not get the chance to listen that today, we are divided by politics, religion, ethnicity, and economic status. Changing water into wine, negativism into positivism,e is presented to us by learning of Jesus Christ and His teachings. I think my father preached a pretty good sermon on this matter. Read and enlighten your dark, negative life.

Sermon

As you will recognize, the text is taken from that event in our Lord's life when at a marriage feast in Cana of Galilee. He turned water into wine. "This beginning of miracles did Jesus in Cana of Galilee and manifested forth His glory, and his disciples believed on Him." John 2

It is not the purpose of this sermon to discuss or analyze the miraculous procedure of this event, but nevertheless, a short word should be said about it. A miracle is usually understood to mean an interference with Nature by a supernatural power. Here the wedding feast in Cana, we have in a moments notice, the conversion of water into wine. This miracle proclaims that the God of all wine is present. The vine of one of the blessings sent by God. Every year, as part of the Natural order, God makes wine. He does so by creating a vegetable organism that can turn water, soil, and sunlight into juice, which will become wine under the proper conditions. Thus, in a certain sense, He constantly turns water into wine, for wine, like all drink is but water modified. Once, and in one year only, God, now incarnate, short circuits the process: He makes wine in a moment: uses earthenware jars instead of vegetable fibers to the hold the water. But He uses them to do what He is always doing. The miracle consists of the shortcut, but the event to which it leads is the usual one. If the thing happened, we know that what has come into nature is no anti-Natural spirit, no God who loves tragedy and tears and fasting for their own sake, but the God of Israel who has through all these centuries given us wine to gladden the hearts of men. We must also remember as we proceed with our thoughts that this wine was of extraordinary quality and value and that our Lord made enough at the moment so that there would be plenty of <u>all</u>.

Now there is an allegorical thought behind this miracle which warrants our attention. We see it not only in the light of this single event but also in the two which follow it: our Lord purging the temple and His insistence to Nicodemus that men must experience a rebirth. To me, they all teach the same thing: Christ changes Judaism into Christianity. The Jews had only water -- but Christ gave them wine -- so He manifested His glory, and His disciples believed on Him.

The allegorical truth portrayed in these events is found in the wine, which is positive spiritual life contrasted with the water or negative ceremonial illustrations. Not only Judaism but Christianity has been content with the water pots or ritual cleansing, centering religion around abstinence and taboos. But a genuine Christian experience is wholly different; it is to have life and have it more abundantly. This life is gained through faithful contact with Christ.

In order to bring men into the fuller life, Christ did not and could not withdraw Himself from the common path and settings of men. He mingled with and purified the daily life of men, to bring out the glory which was everywhere hidden there. And for this, He was called a "winebibber and a glutton."

The historical Jewish religious life was based on a negative approach to all things religious. The fuller life was found not in doing but in not doing. The Book of Leviticus, the law book of the Hebrew people, is full of the "Thou shalt nots." The entire approach to God was set up on the basis of physical actions. It was a matter of various types of offerings, of clean and unclean meats, rites and sacrifices, social activities among the peoples, eschewing the heathen, and ritual practices of the priests. The young Jewish boys hung a tablet around their necks and carried them at all times so that they might learn the law of their fathers. The whole ritualistic system was based upon action rather than on the spirit. But Christ turned the water of negativism of ceremonial lustrations into the twine of positive spiritual life in which the gifts of God are accepted with joy. With the new teachings about God, there came an understanding that it is not action that counted but the thought behind the action. "Except your righteousness shall exceed the righteousness of the scribes and Pharisees, ye shall in no case enter into the kingdom of Heaven." Religion now becomes a positive thing.

"When a man is obeying a law, he is always tempted to do not more than the law requires. The law marks the limits beyond which he may not go, but so long as he remains safely within limits, he is unlikely to be exposed either to censor or punishment. The life of the Jews was meticulously regulated by law. Not only their civil life but their religious and moral life as well was outlined by law so that the Jew was in constant danger of making his total response to life in terms of obedience. Jesus pointed to five specific instances in which the standard set by obedience to the law is immediately raised when once a man sees and appreciates the spirit of God the Father.

The law said that a man must not murder, that he must not commit adultery, that he must keep his sworn contracts, that he must retaliate only in kind, and that he must do well by his neighbor. These five rules the minimum requirements of the Hebrew's life. The least that could be asked of a man was that he not kill another man, nor run away with another man's wife, that he keep his promise, give back no worse than he got and be descent to this next-door neighbor. So long as a man conceived of his moral life in terms of doing what he was told to do for fear of being punished if he did otherwise, he reached his moral goal.

But not so with the man who had made an allegiance, who saw the spirit of God. His goal was immediately changed from the least that the law asked of him to the most that God could expect of him. Murder, adultery, perjury, vengeance, and unneighborliness were ruled out from the start as gross violations of their social life. But so were anger and bitterness ruled out, for they might be more insidiously dangerous to life than murder itself. So were the impure mind and the lust-ridden imagination ruled out, for they were even more subtle exploitations of personal dignity than the more obvious act of adultery. So were oaths sworn under God ruled out, for they implied that the truth could be side-stepped if God's guarantee had not been set upon it. So were resentment and revenge ruled out, for they were signs of a poisoned spirit. So were unfriendliness and unneighborliness ruled out not only on those who were favorably disposed toward each other but also among those who are avowed enemies.

In other words, once a man saw for himself the vision of a God who had created all men and had invested something of Himself in each of them, of a God whose nature and being are to love and to love impartially, once a man had grasped the concept of humanity as the family of God in which each member is of equal worth though not always of equal importance, at that moment the religious and moral standard was raised from the minimum requirements of the least to nothing less than perfection itself. Jesus spoke directly to the heart and mind of every man. He truly turned the water of the negative religious life into the wine of positive spiritual living.

St. Paul was caught in this same dilemma of the negative versus the positive. As a Pharisee, he fiercely resented Jesus' attitude toward the law. He was reared in a Pharisaic home and later trained as a rabbi at the feet of the famous Gamaliel in Jerusalem. But his inner experience was one of profound dissatisfaction and unrest, owing to the conflict between desire and outward conduct. The gist of all this for him was the Divine Law sounding "Thou shalt not" in his heart when desire prompted him toward indulgences of the flesh in some form or another. That was a terrible paradox, but its full misery lay in this, that the law thereby proved in his sinner's experience not the means of deliverance or salvation which pharisaism assumed to be, but rather, the means of more profound condemnation for his complicity with the law of sin in the flesh. That is, the holy law, which ideally was given by God to be "unto life," did, in fact, owing to the pathological condition of man as he is, work unto death. The result of Paul's passionate effort to reach this peace of conscious harmony with God's will by the aid of God's law was summed up in the despairing cry, "Who shall deliver me." And the one answer he found, in the end was "Thank you, Jesus Christ, our Lord."

So Paul's filial type of devotion to the heavenly Father was the very essence of real obedience that of the undivided will of the inner man and became the standard by which the legal system of obedience, which did not unite the heart in complete loyalty, must be judged. In a word, Jesus' holiness was one in the spirit, even when not in the letter also; and he himself was the inspirer of the similar free loyalty in others, as a "life-giving spirit."

So you see, the common problem for us in this day is to transmute life, to find inspiration for it, to change not its content but the meaning of its content, to take its "Two or three firkins of water and make wine of them; that is, to turn what is commonplace and prosaic into what is beautiful, good and true. This is what Jesus did; for example, by His very spirit, he transformed poverty into something bearable. Silver and gold? He had none. But in His very poverty, He came close to the poor and dispensed spiritual gifts of mercy and service like a king. Jesus transformed loneliness. "The son of man hath not where to lay His head." But He made the countryside of Galilee His home and had His sanctuary in the hearts of those who loved him. Jesus transformed suffering by the way He suffered and tasted death for every man by the way He died. Yes, Christ turned the water of ceremonial lustrations into the wine of positive spiritual life in which the gifts of God are accepted with joy.

Given St. Mark's Church, Moscow, Idaho and Palouse, Idaho, January 23, 1949 and January 27, 1952

John, Author of the Gospel

The author of the Gospel According to John is unknown to us in modern times, although the debate continues that it may be the beloved disciple of Jesus. The writer espouses at the end of the Gospel that he was an eyewitness. The Synoptic Gospels, Matthew, Mark and Luke make no claim to eyewitnessing Jesus' life.

For centuries scholars have studied the words, comparing the four Gospels, and the differences are stark. While Matthew, Mark, and Luke begin after the arrest of John the Baptist, the Gospel of John includes many events prior to the arrest. Another difference in the writings seems to indicate that this Gospel was written after the Synoptic Gospels which would make John's claim to be an eyewitness an impossibility.

John writes of a ministry that may have lasted two or three years, whereas the other three claim Jesus' ministry lasted about a year. He knew the area in which Jesus lived as he described places that have archeological evidence. Jesus may have visited Jerusalem more than once unlike the writings of the other three who claim he visited one time.

The historical facets of John's Gospel describe the crucifixion of Jesus with more accuracy than the Synoptic Gospels. John explains that the last supper was not a Passover meal but more likely before Passover which began on Friday. John wrote that Jesus was handed over for crucifixion on the day of Preparation of Passover Week. Many scholars state that this timing may be more accurate than thinking the Sanhedren would meet on the day of Passover.

Whether or not the author of the Gospel was the "beloved Disciple" or a person who came after the writers Matthew, Mark, and Luke, the simple truth remains, the Gospel was important. As the adoption by various Christian followers of the book that became known as the Bible debated many sources of information about Jesus, one thing is clear the early bishops of Christianity believed John wrote an important document.

Biography of Peter Stockwell

Peter Stockwell is a retired middle school teacher embarking on his next career telling stories. After 32 years of guiding minds and emotions of preteen and teenage students, he left the classroom to relax and enjoy the rest of his life with family and friends. Instead, he wrote a book and published it. The fun began when he learned the next step, marketing his creation to the world. He has now written eight books with several more in the future.

He lives with his wife, Sandy, and two cats in Silverdale, Washington. He has five children and eight grandchildren who are a source of great joy. He is member of Pacific Northwest Writers Association (PNWA), International Thriller Writers (ITW), and Northwest Independent Writer Association (NIWA) and Kitsap Literary Artists & Writers (KLAW). He publishes through Westridge Art, a company he founded.

Compiling his father's sermons into a series of books has been a loving undertaking to honor the words that invigorate humanity. The sermons are to be shared by anyone who wants or needs an inspiration. Each compilation and wirtten commentary are developed to continue the teachings of Jesus Christ as given in the sermons of the Reverend Norman Stockwell.

Each month Peter and Mark Miller, fellow member of KLAW, record and produce a television show in which they interview northwest authors, artists, musicians, and publishers. Production of the show is in conjunction with Bremerton Kitsap Access Television (BKAT).

Contact Peter at stockwellpa@wavecable.com
Follow Peter on Facebook, Instagram, and Twitter

Other books by Peter Stockwell

Mystery series

Motivations
A Story of Love, Family, Betrayal, and Redemption

Motive
A Detective Marcus Jefferson Investigation

Jerry's Motives
The story of Marcus Jefferon's Uncle

Death Stalks Mr. Blackthorne
A Detective Marcus Jefferson Novel

In the Garden of Eden
A Detective Marcus Jefferson Investigation

Science Fiction Series

The Mistress - A Novel

The Android Dawn (coming soon)

The Android Incursion (coming soon)

Non-Fiction

Stormin' Norman
Volume 1

Stormin' Norman
Volume 2

www.ingramcontent.com/pod-product-compliance
Lightning Source LLC
Chambersburg PA
CBHW050444010526
44118CB00013B/1666